MW00528502

God Loves Your Work

God Loves Your Work

Discover Why He Sends You to Do What You Do

Larry Peabody

WIPF & STOCK · Eugene, Oregon

GOD LOVES YOUR WORK
Discover Why He Sends You to Do What You Do

Wipf & Stock
An Imprint of Wipf and Stock Publishers
199 W. 8th Ave., Suite 3
Eugene, OR 97401

www.wipfandstock.com

PAPERBACK ISBN: 978-1-6667-9501-1
HARDCOVER ISBN: 978-1-6667-9499-1
EBOOK ISBN: 978-1-6667-9502-8

02/22/22

Contents

Preface

IT TOOK YEARS BEFORE I discovered that my early Christian education was missing a vitally important piece.

My farmer dad, who loved the Lord, taught me *how* to work—for which I'll always be profoundly grateful. But he never explained the biblical *why* for my work. Our church made it clear *why* missionaries and pastors work. But it did not spell out the *why* behind the work other people do: engineers, grocery checkers, accountants, receptionists, attorneys, garbage collectors, bus drivers, farmers, and so on.

It wasn't until I left home and began wrestling with the direction my life should take that I began to search for the *why* behind non-church work. To my surprise, I found God has not just one or two but many reasons for our daily work. Discovering those reasons took time. But I began to realize that unless I knew God's intent for my work, a major part of my life would remain spiritually meaningless. How could I spend year after year doing work that mattered little or not at all to God?

As Christians, we're motivated to please God. We want his "Well done!" in every area of our lives. So each of us must know God's *why* for the everyday work we do—whether we're paid for it or not. Because I believe in that *must* so strongly, for the past eight years, through the Bakke Graduate University, I have led classes on what God has revealed about our work.

Watching how a biblical understanding of daily work has transformed and brought joy to my students has encouraged me to write this book. As I write these words, I do so for all Christ followers, but especially for four particular groups:

First, this book is for *young people*—those still in school. My own early Christian education lacked any teaching on why God sends his people into the world's workplaces. Sadly, a great many young people today—without knowing it—still begin with the same deficit.

Over the past eight years, I have asked students in my theology-of-work courses to conduct surveys among Christians who work in non-church jobs. Accumulated responses now total more than a thousand. One question asks respondents if they, before entering their life's work, received any biblical instruction how to choose it. Nearly three-quarters say no.

Second, these chapters are for *those now entering the world of work*. I have lost track of how many times participants in my seminars and classes have said, "I wish I had heard this teaching thirty years ago." Think of the difference it would make if, at the outset of their working lives, Christians committed intentionally themselves and their daily work to carrying out God's kingdom purposes here on earth.

Third, I am writing for *those already established in the so-called "secular" workforce* but who struggle to see God's purposes in what they do. Far too many of us are not wholeheartedly engaged in our work. Instead, we try to squeeze all ministry and worship into weekends. We may pine for the day we retire, when—we imagine—we will devote ourselves fully to serving the Lord.

Finally, this book is for *those who receive no paychecks* for their work. What they do is just as important in maintaining life on earth as the work of others who work for wages or salaries. An obvious example of work not compensated monetarily is that of a stay-at-home parent. The value of caring for children and a household cannot be calculated in dollars. But it is absolutely essential if life is to thrive on God's earth.

Whichever of these four groups you may be in, I pray that this book will help you to reframe your thinking about work within a kingdom-of-God perspective, his will being done on earth as in heaven. And I hope that, as a result, you will transform your everyday work, the work itself—not just the money you earn from it—into true ministry and an offering pleasing to God.

Introduction

Bryan and Denise began following Jesus shortly after they were married. At first, the issue did not bother them, because life in Christ was so much better than what they had known before. They loved Jesus and wanted above all to please him. But a couple of years into their Christian lives, something seemed wrong.

Both had great jobs. Denise worked as an accountant in a company that made and installed windows. Bryan, a pilot, flew passenger jets for a commercial airline. Their work lives were the sort others envied. But both Bryan and Denise began feeling like they ought to be investing the hours of their lives in something more spiritually worthwhile.

This vacuum led them to spend long hours evenings and weekends volunteering in church programs. This still didn't seem to satisfy. So they began thinking about going to Tanzania as missionaries. Once there, they reasoned, they would finally be able to serve God in their work full time—not just during off-duty hours. However, their missionary dreams never materialized, so they agreed to wait until they retired. Then, they could really serve God all the way.

Drop in different names, and this story fits the experience of far too many Christ followers. If people like Bryan and Denise were to ask me for advice, I would tell them: *God loves the work you are doing right now.*

Does it trouble you to think that God loves your work? If so, that's not surprising. All of us have heard repeatedly the truth that God loves people. A blog headline offers "20 Inspiring Bible Verses About God's Amazing Love for You."[1] The first of the Four Spiritual Laws says, "God loves you and has a wonderful plan for your life."[2] It's true! God loves you.

To say that God loves *you* won't raise any eyebrows. But to suggest that God loves *your work* takes some explaining. The chapters of this book will, I hope, make it clear how God can and does—in addition to loving you—love your work as well.

Right off, let's be clear: saying God loves your work does not always mean he wants you to stay in the job you now hold. He may lead you to change employment. But if what you do is in some way helping life on his earth to flourish, God loves your work.

A major reason we Christians might find "God loves your work" so troubling has to do with a persistent falsehood our religious traditions keep telling us. This notion proclaims some work is "sacred" or "spiritual," while other work is "secular." If you see work in that split-level way, you'll have a hard time thinking God could love so-called "secular work."

This book aims to help clear away the fog created by dividing work into such unbiblical categories.

As these chapters spell out, there is a lot for God to love in your work. Your work mirrors him, honors him, helps manage his earthly real estate, lets his light shine on earth, blesses the world, and transforms you to be like his Son. As the saying goes, "What's not to love about that?"

This book explores the *what* and the *why* of everyday work—paid or unpaid.

Think of the *what* as the biblical truth-foundation under your work. A foundation supports the building erected on top of it. Having a theological foundation for your everyday work anchors

1. Eng, "20 Inspiring Bible Verses about God's Amazing Love for You."
2. 4Laws.com, "Four Spiritual Laws."

it to your faith in Christ. And it undergirds the biblical reasons for doing it. "Work" is a single-syllable word. So is "cube." At first glance, both seem so simple. But like a cube, work has multiple facets. So we will examine the concept of work from several angles.

How did the whole business of working begin? What value does God see in work? Why is work so often hard and even painful? How can we avoid overworking? What anchor-points connect your work with your faith? What danger lurks in the money made from working? We need biblical answers to these and similar questions.

Think of the *why* as God's purposes for the work that rests on that biblical foundation. Discerning God's reasons for sending you into the world to work will spur you on to do it all—every minute of it—for him.

As a Christ-follower, what should motivate you to get out of bed and go to work? Does your working offer anything spiritually significant enough to keep you at it? Sadly, the great majority of Christians do not learn the *why* in church. In that setting, most rarely hear anything about work. This lack of work-talk makes it seem that Sundays stand apart from and have little or nothing to do with workdays.

My own search for answers to the *what* and *why* questions about work has taken place through several working roles. I have worked as a wage-earner, a salaried employee, a business owner, a church planter, a senior pastor, and a grad school professor teaching the theology of work. So I have firsthand experience in many kinds of work. In this book, I aim to communicate the great difference it makes when we understand that God loves not only us but also our daily work.

I pray that this book will help you begin to build a biblical foundation for the work you do between Sundays. And may it help you to discover a whole new level of motivation for whatever it is you do.

Note: A brief "Discussion" section, with questions, follows each chapter. You may use these on your own or with a group. At the end of each chapter, you'll also find a "For more" notation that offers a reading suggestion that will provide further material on the subject.

1

He Started It!

I GREW UP WITH dirty hands. My work as a farm boy—planting, weeding, harvesting—got my hands grimy. Often, after I had pulled weeds all day, the stains in my fingers could be removed only with bleach. The work of mechanics, roofers, and painters leaves their hands a mess, too. They may have to clean up with industrial-strength hand cleaners.

What about God? Do his hands ever get dirty?

God's Dirty Work

Okay, I don't think God has physical thumbs and fingers. Even so, the Bible speaks time after time about his hands. The story of God getting his hands dirty begins in the Genesis account of creation. That narrative leaves no doubt that God is not above such work.

Have you noticed whenever you read the story that God did not make Adam like he made everything else? He said, "Let there be light," but did not say, "Let there be a man." No. Instead, God *formed* Adam. That verb suggests squeezing into a shape—as a child might shape a cookie out of Play-Doh.

But God didn't use modeling clay. He picked up some dust. Plain old earth-dirt. Then, after forming Adam, God—working like a surgeon—opened a wound in Adam's flesh, removed a rib, and made Eve. God's messy work didn't end there. In another task, instead of delegating the grubby work to an angel, he himself planted a garden.

From farm-boy experience, I know planting gets done in dirt. And later, after his human creatures ignored his clear instructions, God took on the task of a tailor or leatherworker. He made clothes for them out of what must have been blood-soaked animal skins. The point? Right from the start of the Bible, God reveals himself to be a worker.

The Demeaning of Work

Think of the working people you know. How would you describe their typical attitude toward work? Is it an irritating interruption between weekends? Do they see it as just a way to bring home enough money to pay for what they *really* want to have and to do? Is the job merely an annoying nuisance to put up with until retirement?

This whole idea that work is a bother may well trace back to what ancient Greeks thought about working. Their culture launched much of what we take for granted today. Philosophy. Mathematics. Juries. Even democracy. Another hand-me-down from the Greeks was their attitude toward work.

The Greek gods saw work as degrading. One writer says, instead of working, they partied, plotted and warred against each other, and made love. Someone else has written, "Hypnos . . . is the one whose mantra is '*less work and more sleep*.'"[1]

This attitude of their gods seeped into the way the Greeks saw work. And no wonder. As the Bible explains, "those who make idols are just like them, as are all who trust in them" (Ps 135:18, NLT). So if the fake gods of the Greeks wanted to avoid hard and dirty work, those who worshiped them saw work that way too.

1. Sengupta, "7 Greek Gods and Goddesses."

Even their philosophers, like Plato and Aristotle, saw work—especially with one's hands—as something unfit for human beings.

The True God Works

But long before those Greeks invented their phony, lazy gods, the true God had revealed himself to the Hebrew people as a working God—a God willing to get his hands dirty. Jesus, the God-Man, was born into the home of a manual laborer, learned the trade, and wore calluses on his hands. He later clinched the truth that God is a worker when he said, "My Father is always at his work to this very day, and I too am working" (John 5:17). As Christians, we also become like the One we worship. And so for us, this means all legitimate work, whether with hands or head, paid or unpaid, carries honor and dignity. Why? Because it reflects the all-wise Maker of everything.

I recently taught a course on living out faith in the workplace for a church in a neighboring town, In the first session, one of the women in the class said, "It never occurred to me to go back to Genesis to see how work began." Does a lack of focus on Genesis explain why this God-as-Worker truth catches many Christians by surprise? Our Bibles begin with these five words: "In the beginning God created . . ." Word 4 tells us God *exists*. Word 5 tells us he *works*.

Tim Keller and Katherine Leary Alsdorf open chapter 1 of their book *Every Good Endeavor* by saying, "The Bible begins talking about work as soon as it begins talking about anything—that is how important and basic it is. The author of the book of Genesis describes God's creation of the world as *work*."[2]

Well, yes, someone may object, "But the work God did must have been far easier for him than the hassles I put up with day after day, week after week, and year after year. God didn't have to cope with cranky bosses, crashing hard drives, and absurd deadlines."

2. Keller and Alsdorf, *Every Good Endeavor*, 33.

True. But what God did still qualifies as work. Webster defines the noun "work" as "activity in which one exerts strength or faculties to do or perform something."[3] Certainly God exerted both his strength and his faculties in creating the heavens and the earth. And in doing so, he performed something. So—if we define it like that—God did indeed work.

Work Is Good

I have taught faith-at-work classes online for several years. My students have come from many countries. Some have been told by their Christian leaders that God needed a way to punish sinful people—and so he came up with work. God's curse, these Christians were told, launched work. So they learned early on to connect work with sin. Yes, they must work to pay the bills and feed their families. But working in a so-called "secular" job leaves them with an uneasy conscience.

Knowing God as First Worker can free us up. Why? Because seeing him that way corrects a lot of disabling ideas about work. If God is totally good (and he is), and if the totally good God works (and he does), then working itself must be good. But work is not always understood that way—not even by Christians.

Work Can Bring Joy

It's freeing to know that work is good because the good God works. But there's a second benefit that comes from knowing God as Worker. While the Bible doesn't say it in so many words, it gives us good reason to believe that God actually relishes working. If you read the Genesis creation story, you'll see that as God is creating, he pauses at least four times, looks over the results of his work, and says, "It's good." And when the project is all done, he pauses again and says, "It's *very* good." God takes real pleasure in his work and what it produces.

3. Merriam-Webster Online, "Work."

In Proverbs 8 we hear Wisdom speaking. Wisdom thinks back to all the work God did in creation. Then Wisdom speaks: "I was the architect at his side. I was his constant delight, rejoicing always in his presence. And how happy I was with the world he created; how I rejoiced with the human family!" (Prov 8:30–31, NLT). Can you hear the joy in the voice of Wisdom, God's "architect"? Knowing God as Worker lets us see that working can bring joy.

It's likely that many long-time Christian friends of yours don't know God has revealed himself to be a Worker. How can you help them see that truth? Here's an idea. Next time you are hanging out with some Christians, play a game that goes like this: Ask them this question: "How many examples can you think of where the Bible describes what God does by comparing him with some kind of human worker?"

I'll give you just one example to get you started. Hebrews 11:10 speaks of God as an architect. I'd give you more examples, but I don't want to spoil the fun with your friends.

The Work of God—A Major Theme in Scripture

After playing that game with your friends, you and they may want to take on another challenge. Using a concordance, search for "work," "works," and "deeds." Then look up the verses that speak of these as the activity of God or the Lord. The sheer number of verses may astonish you.

When Bible people like David and the other Psalmists praised God, they did not stop with words like "awesome," "great," "amazing," and "wonderful." Such adjectives sometimes appeared. But when those pioneers of faith worshiped the Lord, they filled their praises with references to the work God did and does. Here are a few samples, just from the Psalms:

- "When I consider your heavens, the work of your fingers, the moon and the stars, which you have set in place . . ." (8:3).
- "They will proclaim the works of God and ponder what he has done" (64:9).

- "Say to God, 'how awesome are your deeds'" (66:3).
- "I declare your marvelous deeds" (71:17).
- "I will meditate on all your works and consider all your mighty deeds" (77:12).
- "Praise the Lord, all his works everywhere in his dominion" (103:22).
- "Let them sacrifice thank offerings and tell of his works with songs of joy" (107:22).
- "The works of his hands are faithful and just" (111:7).

So the fact that God is a worker launched biblical worshipers into praise—pondering on and naming what he had done, what he still does, and what he will yet do.

God Accepts Our Work

Knowing that work originated in God himself assures us that he very much approves the act of working. Our work is not something he just stuck in as a filler to keep us busy between Sundays. Even the kinds of work our culture labels as "dirty jobs" (as in the TV series) are pleasing to God.

As already noted, Jesus worked as a carpenter or builder. He coped with sawdust, skinned fingers, splinters, and other irksome workplace events. Paul, Priscilla, and Aquila made tents from animal skins—a messy, smelly business. Peter and other apostles caught and sold fish—getting soaked as they hauled in each netful of the slippery creatures.

Nothing in Scripture even hints that these hand-intensive, dirty jobs were unacceptable to God the Worker. In short, we may offer any kind of legitimate work up to him.

New Creation: God's Greatest Work

As we've seen, God himself got his hands dirty in the work of creation. But he later set about even messier work. We human beings, the pinnacle of his first magnificent work, have been twisted and fractured by sin. The image of himself God had embedded in each of us got mangled and warped.

And so God set about a work even greater than that of his first creation—the restoring work of new creation. Jesus, God the Son, took on this painful, grubby, blood-spattered work on the cross. There, he took all our failure on himself. He did so to make us clean and whole. And so, once again, God demonstrated that he was not afraid to soil his hands for us, this time getting his own nailed hands dirty with our corruption.

It took dirty work for God to create us in his first creation. And it took even dirtier work to restore us. Aren't you glad our God, unlike those Greek gods, is a Worker?

In his new creation, we are "being transformed into his image" (2 Cor 3:18). As a result, we are regaining our ability to reflect our Creator to his world—and to do so through our work.

Discussion

1. How do Genesis 2:2–3 add to the evidence that God is a worker?
2. Did reading this chapter expand your understanding of God? If so, how?
3. How does knowing God as a worker give you confidence that he will accept your work as an offering?

For more: Banks, Robert. *God the Worker: Journeys into the Mind, Heart, and Imagination of God*. Eugene, OR: Wipf & Stock, 2008.

2

God-Reflectors

TRAVEL WHEREVER YOU WILL on earth and you'll find folks working: harvesting sugarcane in Nepal, cutting marble slabs in Italy, or gathering eiderdown in Iceland to fill duvets. People around the world engage in an endless variety of work. In 2020, the global workforce totaled an estimated 3.4 billion people. Although work began with God, it spread like a grassfire all around the planet. Just in Genesis alone we read of those who worked as shepherds, cattle farmers, vineyard keepers, bakers, city-builders, toolmakers, musicians, and government officials.

Why? What explains such a universal practice of people getting up and heading off to work?

The answer is packed densely into the language of Genesis. So it takes observant reading to see why work, beginning with God, branched out to include the entire human community. Here are the jam-packed-with-meaning words from Genesis 1:26:

"Then God said, 'Let us make mankind in our image, in our likeness, so that they may rule . . .'"

As part of his work, God had set about making human beings. But he decided not just to add another species of animal. Instead, he fashioned these creatures in his own "image" or "likeness." An image or likeness serves what purpose? If you ask an artist to paint a likeness of your daughter, you want the portrait to reflect her accurately. Anyone looking at it should catch a glimpse of her beauty and charm. In a similar but living way, you and I were made to be God-reflectors.

Take care not to miss the connection inside Genesis 1:26. *Why* did God create us to serve him as God-reflectors? What about him are we to reflect? "Let us make mankind in our image . . . so that they may rule." Until he made mankind, God had been ruling, completely in charge of making and running things—*working*. Now, God was sharing with human beings his work of ruling. This work would be the foundational way they would reflect him on earth—the work of ruling his earth under his oversight.

The post-sin world system, however—instead of encouraging us to work as God-reflectors—presses us to work as money-makers. A blog post headline asks, "*How Much Money Do You Need to Never Have to Work Again?*" Another headline promises to tell you, "*How to Live Off Dividends and Never Have to Work Again.*" Both bloggers are making two big (and mistaken) assumptions. One—ditching work is a good thing. And two—work is all about making money.

Which brings us to the question:

Why Work?

Many American males have not found any good answer to that question. In his 2015 book, *Men without Work: America's Invisible Crisis*, Nicholas Eberstadt tells the story. Backed up by mountains of statistical evidence, he reports that, "By 2015, the number of prime-age inactive men was over 7 million—6.5 times higher than it had been a half-century earlier." Eberstadt calls this species of male "the un-working American man."[1]

1. Eberstadt, *Men without Work*, 32.

"For un-working men," he says, "watching TV and movies ate up an average of five and a half hours a day."[2] How do these guys eat and pay the bills? "Relatives and friends and the US government float these long-term nonparticipants in the workforce."[3] Eberstadt found that these non-working men lived "on the largesse of women they knew and taxpayers they did not."[4] What keeps them from finding a job? "One critical determinant to being in the US workforce today seems to be wanting to be there in the first place."[5]

These millions of unworking American men can get their hands on money without working. So it seems that for them even making money is not a sufficient answer to the "Why work?" question. Among people who *are* working, a great many hold their jobs just to pay the bills. Making an income is one God-given benefit of working, but it should not be the only or even the main motive for getting out of bed and clocking in on the job.

So, then, back again to that persistent question:

Why Work?

This time, let's approach the question by digging a little more deeply into what we covered in chapter 1. We saw that the true God—in contrast to those work-shirking Greek gods—is a Worker.

As the final touch, the capstone, of his creating work, God made human beings. In many ways, our bodies are like those of animals—flesh, bones, nerves, blood, and so on. But in one way, we're completely *unlike* animals: you and I are made to be like God. As already noted, he created us "in his image."

Immediately after he made the human beings, the working God began assigning work for *them* to do. "Be fruitful and multiply," he said. "Fill the earth and govern it. Reign over the fish in the sea, the birds in the sky, and all the animals that scurry along

2. Eberstadt, *Men without Work*, 65.

3. Eberstadt, *Men without Work*, 93.

4. Eberstadt, *Men without Work*, 94.

5. Eberstadt, *Men without Work*, 56.

the ground" (Gen 1:28, NLT). So God the Worker wanted human workers all round his planet to reflect him. People who, in their working, would mirror him to the world.

Keeping in mind our design as God-reflecting earth-rulers, let's look at four ways to answer the question: "Why work?"

1. We Work to Show What God Is Like

By working, we reflect into the world a picture of the working God. Refuse to work and you short-change the world of a small portrait of the God who works. Worse, if—as an able-bodied adult—you reject working and simply loaf around, living off the efforts of others, you're actually misrepresenting God, projecting a false picture of him.

A problem like that surfaced among the Christians in the first-century city of Thessalonica. Some of them were dodging work. When Paul wrote to the believers in that church, he urged them to "keep away from every brother who is idle." He pointed to himself as an example: "We were not idle when we were with you." Paul, whose calloused hands came from cutting and sewing leather for tents, added, "We worked night and day, laboring and toiling so that we would not be a burden to any of you" (2 Thess 3:7–8).

Why did Paul see a non-working lifestyle as unthinkable? Because he knew God as the working God. The Old Testament brims over with passages about God and his work.

- Moses asks God, "What god is there in heaven or on earth who can do the deeds and mighty works you do?" (Deut 3:24).
- Job challenges his friends to consider the skies, clouds, moon, oceans, light, and darkness, and reminds them, "these are but the outer fringe of his works" (Job 26:14).
- David stands awestruck before the Worker God: "Come and see what God has done, how awesome his works in man's behalf!" (Ps 66:5).

And Paul must have known that Jesus described both his Father and himself as workers: "My Father is always at his work to this very day, and I, too, am working" (John 5:17). The first disciples sometimes went hungry as a result of Jesus' working. As Mark comments, "So many people were coming and going that they did not even have a chance to eat" (Mark 6:31). And John records words from Jesus that indicate the urgency that kept him at it: "As long as it is day, we must do the work of him who sent me. Night is coming, when no one can work" (John 9:4).

So when we work, we offer the world a small display of what the true God is like. In that way, our work serves as a signpost pointing to God and his work.

2. *We Work to Echo God's Generosity*

The first answer to the "Why work?" question: to mirror the activity of the working God. Second, by working, we reflect the giving nature of the working God. Jesus said, "Give, and it will be given to you. A good measure, pressed down, shaken together and running over, will be poured into your lap" (Luke 6:38). In saying this, Jesus emphasized God's liberality.

Paul describes God as the one "who richly provides us with everything for our enjoyment." He follows that up immediately by telling Timothy to teach well-off Christians to mirror that characteristic of God: "Command them to do good, to be rich in good deeds, and to be generous and willing to share" (1 Tim 6:17–18).

Paul's words explain how it is possible for us to reflect God's generosity in our sharing with others. That kind of reflection flows through "good deeds," literally good works. In other words, by working. In his book *Work: The Meaning of Your Life*, Lester DeKoster says: "Work is the form in which we make ourselves useful to others."[6]

6. DeKoster. *Work: The Meaning of Your Life*, 1.

DeKoster continues: "No work? Then nothing else either. Culture and civilization don't just happen. They are made to happen and to keep happening—by God the Holy Spirit, *through our work*."[7]

How will we come to have something to give? Only by producing something. As Paul told the Christians in Ephesus, "He who has been stealing must steal no longer, but must work, doing something useful with his own hands, that he may have something to share with those in need" (Eph 4:28). Our generosity flows not only through giving money earned but also through the products and services that result from our work.

3. *We Work to Live Out Our Design*

So we work to mirror the activity of the working God and to reflect his generosity. Third, by working—even if not in an ideal job—we fulfill what we were designed to do. We Christians are, as Ephesians 2:10 assures us, "created in Christ Jesus to do good works."

God recognizes all kinds of work as "good." But as flawed human beings, we often use false pecking orders to upgrade or downgrade work. Mental work trumps manual work. Missionary work gets an A, while the report card for "secular" shows a C or D. White-collar work racks up more bragging points than blue-collar work.

But because all legitimate work reflects our Godlikeness, it confers a sense of self-respect on those who do it. Even those in what society considers demeaning jobs find in them a dignity that has nothing to do with their ranking in the cultural caste system.

Back in the early 1970s, Studs Terkel—how's that for a name?—interviewed more than 130 Americans for his book, *Working*. His subtitle tells it all: *People Talk about What They Do All Day and How They Feel about What They Do*. His research made clear to him that "work is a search for daily meaning as well

7. DeKoster. *Work: The Meaning of Your Life*, 2.

as for daily bread."[8] Terkel found that even what we consider to be the lowest of low jobs gave people stature and self-respect.

For example, Terkel spoke with a gravedigger who had not gone even to grade school. The man told Terkel,

> Not anybody can be a gravedigger . . . A gravedigger, you have to make a neat job. I had a fella once, he wanted to see a grave. He was a fella that digged sewers. He was impressed when he seen me digging this grave—how square and how perfect it was. A human body is goin' into this grave. That's why you need skill when you're gonna dig a grave . . . A gravedigger is a very important person. You must have hear' about the strike we had in New York about two years ago. There were twenty thousand bodies layin' and nobody could bury 'em.[9]

This man, by working—even digging graves—enjoyed the dignity of doing something God had designed him to be able to do.

Let's review. Why work? One, to reflect the activity of the working God. Two, to mirror the generosity of the working God. And three, to fulfill what we were designed to do. But there's one more answer to the "Why work?" question—one so basic and important we dare not overlook it.

4. We Work to Obey God

Finally, we work to do what the working God tells us to do (more on this in chapter 13.) In the Fourth Commandment, God says, "Six days you shall labor and do all your work." And a bit later in that same commandment comes the reason behind this command: "For in six days the Lord made the heavens and the earth, the sea, and all that is in them" (Exod 20:11). This command makes working an act of obedience.

Essentially, God is saying, "You are to work because I do." Why work? Because by working, you mirror the working God in

8. Terkel, *Working*, xi.

9. Terkel, *Working*, 507, 509.

his activity and generosity. And that is exactly what he designed you to do. In obeying God's command to work, you discover dignity and meaning.

John Stott, a British theologian, defined work in these words: "Work is the expenditure of energy (manual or mental or both) in the service of others, which brings fulfillment to the worker, benefit to the community, and glory to God."[10] Work like that makes an offering in which God delights.

Sadly, though, early in human history sin burst into the world and struck work with a severe blow.

Discussion

1. What would the world lack if no one did the kind of work you do?
2. Think back on the reasons for working described in this chapter. How are these superior to the typical reasons the world-system offers?
3. In what ways can the work you do serve as an offering?

For more: Chapter 4 of Cosden, Darell. *The Heavenly Good of Earthly Work*. Peabody, MA: Hendrickson, 2006.

10. Stott, *Issues Facing Christians Today*, 225.

3

God Rescues Work

"I GO TO WORK in tears every day because I hate my job!" A tearful woman who phoned into the Ken Coleman show sobbed out these words.[1]

Studs Terken introduces his book, *Working*, like this:

> This book, being about work, is by its very nature about violence—to the spirit as well as to the body. It is about ulcers as well as accidents, about shouting matches as well as fistfights, about nervous breakdowns as well as kicking the dog around . . . To survive the day is triumph enough for the walking wounded among the great many of us.[2]

Work Suffers

Visualize how the man found by the Samaritan in Jesus' parable might have looked before and after he was attacked by robbers. Pre-sin and post-sin pictures of work would also show a change

1. Ken Coleman Show, "I Go to Work in Tears Every Day Because I Hate My Job!"

2. Terkel, *Working*, xi.

for the worse. Like the victim in Jesus' parable, work was originally strong and healthy—a good gift from God. But once sin entered the world, work took a beating.

Some people see work as God's punishment for eating from the off-limits tree. But God did not curse work. He cursed the *ground.* As a result, it began sprouting plants covered with sharp, spiky projections. Skin piercers. These plants took over space in the soil and used up valuable water. But they produced nothing edible.

Imagine trying to raise a garden or harvest crops in that weed-infested ground. So even though work itself was never cursed, the cursed ground made work far more difficult, frustrating, and exhausting. Just as thieves waylaid the man on his way to Jericho, the curse on the ground—the consequence of sin—maimed the gift of work by defacing it with toil.

Sin corrupted every significant relationship of our lives: with God, with each other, and with the earth. And the injury to every one of those relationships took a toll on our work.

Sin Distanced Us from God

Although the Bible tells us God assigned Adam to work and take care of the Garden, it does not reveal anything about what work was like before sin. But by stitching together other information Scripture does provide, we can make some likely guesses.

God had taken great delight in his earth-property, calling it all—including its human managers—"very good." He had come looking for Adam and Eve when he walked through the Garden in the cool part of the day. This hints that they had enjoyed an open and pleasing relationship with God and that he liked being with them.

Adam and Eve may well have proudly displayed each day's labor before God—like children running to show off their latest artwork to Dad. Did God encourage them in their work with more "Very good!" words? Work in that sinless, weedless world must have been pure delight.

But sin broke off that friend-to-friend relationship with God. Now the embarrassed couple found themselves hiding from God, trying to dodge him. Suddenly, the joy of working to please their Creator had disappeared.

God shaped us to be with him. No wonder, then, that being distant from God degrades every part of our lives, including our work. God intended our work to be done with joy and in fellowship with him. Apart from him, work becomes something to endure and escape from.

When God's property managers, like the prodigal son, separated themselves from him, they found themselves in a "distant country." Sin wrecked their vertical relationship with God (and so with their work). But sin also ruined their horizontal relationships.

Sin Distanced Us from Each Other

Sin pitted the woman against her man. When God told her, "Your desire will be for your husband" (Gen 3:16), he did not mean sexual hunger. The Hebrew word translated as "desire" is the same word God used when he told Cain, sin "desires to have you" (Gen 4:7). In other words, sin wanted to rule Cain. But God told him: "You must rule over it." Cain would have to fight sin and overpower it.

In the same way, under the new sin-arrangement, the man would seek to dominate the woman, and she would push back, wanting to rule over him. That is how sin launched what we now call "the battle of the sexes."

Today's gender wars got their start in Genesis 3. This conflict affects not only the marriages but also the workplaces of the world. Traditionally, women have been devalued in the workplace. They report far more sexual harassment than male workers. The mistreatment of women also gets reflected in earnings for comparable work. In the US in 2021, women reportedly received 83.3 cents for each dollar earned by men.[3]

Men in the workplace also feel the bite of gender warfare. In a New York Times op-ed piece, David Brooks writes: "An increasing number of high school-educated men say they are the ones being

3. Bureau of Labor Statistics, "Usual Weekly Earnings."

screwed by modern society, not women, who are better educated on average. More and more college-educated men . . . [argue] that the assault on 'male privilege' has gone too far, that the feminist speech and behavior codes have gone too far."[4]

By separating us from each other, sin wounded our work.

Sin Disrupted Earth and Work

So in sweeping us away from God and pitting us against fellow human beings, sin robbed joy from work. Sin also put us at odds with the earth itself—the setting for our work. As already noted, God did not curse work. Instead, he directed his curse against the ground.

As a result, the planet suffered then—and continues to do so. As Paul explains in Romans 8:20, "the creation was subjected to frustration," was brought into "bondage to decay." And no wonder. The earth's property managers, ourselves made of its dust, had gone AWOL, shirking our earth-keeping role.

This injury to the earth, of course, botched up our work. The cursed earth now began to sprout hurtful things it was never meant to produce—pain-inflicting thorns and thistles. Tending the Garden—once a delight—now became a dreary, even dangerous, chore.

In our post-agricultural age, those thorns and thistles show up as all kinds of stinging workplace nettles. Rivalry. Office politics. Job insecurity. Unreasonable deadlines. Overtime and underpay. Toxic coworkers. Meaningless and repetitive tasks. These are some of the weeds that now infest the twenty-first-century work-world garden. Perhaps thorns and thistles of this sort caused the woman on the Coleman show to blurt out, "I go to work in tears every day because I hate my job!"

Work—the good gift of God—is still good. But sin has made it heavy with trouble.

4. Brooks, "Gender War Is On! And Fake."

Work Recovers

How, for Christ followers, has work recovered? To understand that, we need to return for another look at the damage done by sin. What was lost when sin entered the picture?

Genesis 1 and 2 never refer to God as "King." But that royal word would accurately describe his position and role on earth. Under him, Adam and Eve became God's property managers. Their work involved populating the earth, watching over it, and keeping things in line here on God's real estate. We might think of the human role as that of "prime minister," one who carries out the will of a sovereign.

Sin found its opening when God's earth-rulers stopped taking orders from him, their King. Instead, they began obeying another spirit who came to them in the serpent. That "ancient serpent," as we later learn, "is the devil, or Satan" (Rev 20:2). So those with authority to rule God's earth put themselves under the authority of Satan. As a result, he became the de facto ruler of the earth-rulers.

Satan's power-grab was illegitimate. Even so, Jesus called him—not the king—but the "prince of this world." A prince wields great authority. Paul calls him "ruler of the kingdom of the air" (Eph 2:2). And John tells us "the whole world is under the control of the evil one" (1 John 5:19). And that "whole world" took in the world of work.

When God foretold painful childbirth for the woman's labor and thorns and thistles for the man's work, he was simply announcing the consequences of serving the wrong ruler. Under the rule of the usurper, God's good gift of work, then, turned into something traumatic.

What was lost? The recognition of God's authority. Those God had put in charge of the earth no longer recognized his rule here.

Rightful Authority Restored

But when Jesus died on the cross, something wonderful happened—both for the world and for work. As N. T. Wright makes clear in *How God Became King*, "God really has become king—in and through Jesus!"[5] The Messiah has received "all authority in heaven and on earth" (Matt 28:18). Once again, the King—the rightful King—rules. And in his humanity he represents us, the original earth-rulers.

That rule, Wright says, is now recognized and carried out through those who trust and follow Jesus. They are God's new temple.

> Jesus' followers, equipped with his Spirit, are to become in themselves, individually and together, little walking temples, rescued themselves from sin through Jesus death, and with the living presence of God going with them and in them . . . The dwelling of the living God is now spread increasingly across and around the world, again evidenced not by coercive or violent power, but by the rule of love.[6]

Every workday, millions of these "little walking temples" get up and fan out into shops, offices, schools, homes, hospitals, fields, and workplaces of all sorts. Jesus' followers have themselves been renewed. Through them, Jesus, by his Spirit, carries out his rule of love throughout the world.

But the world and its prince continue their campaign to harass these walking temples. As they work, the prince keeps trying to pull them back under his rule. And just as the earth draws us with its gravity, the world—as if by a magnet—drags us into its clutches. On our own, none of us has the power to stand firm against the world's constant yanking.

John bluntly exposes the power of the world's appeal: "Practically everything that goes on in the world—wanting your own way, wanting everything for yourself, wanting to appear important—has nothing to do with the Father. It just isolates you from him. The world and all its wanting, wanting, wanting is on the way out" (1 John 2:16, MSG). The world of work is crammed with the "weeds" of this wanting.

5. Wright, *How God Became King*, 37.

6. Wright, *How God Became King*, 247–48.

God's remedy in Christ? We who belong to him have died to the world. As Paul told the Galatian believers, " May I never boast except in the cross of our Lord Jesus Christ, through which the world has been crucified to me, and I to the world" (Gal 6:14).

Picture the world as a sleazy salesperson in a flea market shouting to me, even pulling my arm to persuade me to buy this trinket or that doodad. If I happen to want what is being peddled, I am vulnerable to the appeals. But now suppose that I am in a casket being carried past the sales pitches. The loudest and cleverest appeals will have no power to dictate what I do.

Like everything else in the Christian life, this dying with Christ operates through faith. God says we died with Jesus. Do we believe him? Paul told the Roman Christians they were "buried with him through baptism into death" (Rom 6:4). And he urged the Colossian believers to "set your minds on things above, not on earthly things. For you died, and your life is now hidden with Christ in God" (Col 3:2–3).

But God does not leave us there. Through Christ, again, he has brought us to life. By implanting his own Holy Spirit within us, God has "made us alive with Christ" and "raised us up with Christ" (Eph 2:5–6). We are, in the language of the New Testament, now part of God's new creation. This breakthrough into real life right now revolutionizes our relationship with God, with others, and with the earth.

Reunited with God

After God became King again on the cross of Christ, we who receive him are put back into right relationship with him. No more need to hide. Now, our world and our work are set right-side-up again. Just as Adam and Eve must have done, we can now bring all the joys, puzzles, and difficulties of our daily work to him. We know that our work matters to him and that he loves our work.

The good news that God's kingdom has come near in Jesus includes sins forgiven—and much more. The Christmas carol "Joy to the World" says it so well: "No more let sins and sorrows grow, nor thorns infest the ground; He comes to make his blessings flow far as the curse is found."

Yes, those thorns and thistles still sprout up in every workplace. But in Christ the blessings flow over and around them. Consider just two of those blessings: his promise to be with us always and the assurance that "it is the Lord Christ you are serving" (Col 3:24). In other words, even in our daily work, we work alongside God.

So we can again, as in the pre-sin world, do our work in close companionship with God. Work on this decaying planet still presents harsh challenges, But we can again offer each day's labor to our God as a worshipful sacrifice.

Reconciled with Others

The blame game got off to its roaring start when sin drove a wedge between Adam and Eve. The wedge plunged even deeper in the breach between their sons. Cain, on his own farm, murdered his brother—the first instance of workplace violence. The distrust and division between people spread around the globe, a major part of what came to make work painful.

In today's workplaces, most tasks require us to interact with other people just as imperfect as we ourselves are. The triggers of conflict always lie within reach and are easy to pull. But those who have experienced God's forgiveness are themselves given the power to extend grace and to forgive.

Workplace conflicts can distance us from coworkers, bosses, vendors, and so on. As in other areas of life, these on-the-job collisions can usually be summed up by completing this sentence-starter: "You owe me . . ." For example:

"You owe me more respect than to have said what you did."

"You owe me big time for taking credit for my idea."

"You owe me for spreading lies about my competence."

The New Testament gives us a you-owe-me example from a first-century workplace. The crisis comes about when Onesimus, slave to Philemon, runs away. In the Roman Empire, this amounted to much more than an employee walking off the job in crunch time. Slaves were property. Philemon had presumably paid good money to own Onesimus. So in leaving his workplace, Onesimus robbed his boss-owner. Not only that, but his exit left a vacancy in Philemon's work crew.

In his letter to Philemon, Paul acknowledges that the runaway had been "useless" to his owner. If ever there was a you-owe-me situation, this is it. But Paul urges Philemon to "welcome him" back with the same kind of warm welcome he would give to his friend, Paul. Any amount due, Paul promises, he will pay out of his own pocket.

King Jesus calls and empowers his forgiven people to become forgiving people. The distance sin put between ourselves and those we work with has been removed. In Christ—no longer ruled by sin—we have the power to show grace to those who do not deserve it.

In *Kingdom Calling*, Amy Sherman tells about hearing a pastor, Jeff White, compare our calling with "those tiny pink taste-test spoons from Baskin-Robbins . . . Jeff challenged attendees to see themselves as such spoons, for our role in the world is about offering foretastes of the kingdom to our neighbors near and far."[7]

Repossessed for Work

After sin broke into the world, it sheared off our life-giving relationship with God. Sin snarled the lines that connected us with each other. But sin also put us at odds with our role of caring for life on this once-friendly earth.

After putting us right, Jesus sends us back into his world. He calls that world "the field" (Matt 13:38). As already noted, the world-field, which includes the work world, is still full of "thorns and thistles." We ourselves get scratched and jabbed by the barbs and our coworkers experience the same pain. So the irritation

7. Sherman, *Kingdom Calling*, 23.

from those curse-weeds makes the workplace a zone full of tension and potential clashes.

Jesus sends his little walking temples right into that setting. His commission carries us not into some safe, quiet sanctuary but into a battle zone. And there he intends that we engage in the productive work of ruling our assigned sphere of action. As Paul explained to the Christians in Ephesus—many working as slaves—"[God] creates each of us by Christ Jesus to join him in the work he does, the good work he has gotten ready for us to do, work we had better be doing" (Eph 2:10, MSG).

God ruled as King in the Garden of Eden. His will was done on earth as in heaven through the ruling work of human beings. King Jesus now has all authority in heaven and on earth. He rules on earth not by force or compulsion but through those in whom he lives. They represent him in generous acts of love and mercy—even on an earth still reeling from the curse. In this way, as Christ followers do their work, they are able, under the true King, to rule their various spheres on earth.

As Jonathan Nowlen puts it, "When you stand on earth and hold on to heaven, you become a conduit for the culture found in heaven to flow into the garden of earth."[8]

A New Perspective on Pain

Any kingdom-of-God agent working in the world-field will experience grief (those thorns and thistles again). Aiming to see God's will done on earth attracts resistance and even hostility. Here again, because of what Jesus did, our suffering has a purpose. Even he "learned obedience from what he suffered" (Heb 5:8). God's word assures us that, in Christ, the hard times we go through are meant to develop and mature us (see chapter 15).

Some Christ followers, facing trials on the job, have imagined greener grass in so-called full-time Christian service. Burned out in a regular job, they think a church job would be more fulfilling.

8. Nowlen, *Managing Your Metron*, 70.

Or they imagine crossing an ocean to work as a missionary would offer more opportunity to "change the world." Too often, thoughts like these turn out to be fantasies.

The thorns and thistles encountered along the way do not come as signals that we should abandon the work world. We can now see in the trouble more growth opportunities.

Working in Hope

The ground of this old earth still bears God's curse. Work can still hurt. But in Christ, God has reunited us with himself, our life-source. In Christ, our vertical reconciliation makes us able to reach out horizontally to coworkers and others. And in Christ, God has repossessed us for work.

Even as we work, we do so hopefully, working and relating in ways that will allow others to sample life in the kingdom of God yet to come. We can work in the confidence that in the new earth, "No longer will there be any curse" (Rev 22:3). And even now, because in Christ our work has recovered, we can do it in confidence that God accepts it as a worship offering.

Discussion

1. In your work, how have you seen the wedges sin drives between people and God, each other, and the earth itself?
2. What difficulties in your work are evidence of the curse on the ground?
3. In what ways have you experienced God's blessings overflowing the effects of the curse?

For more: Chapter 11 of Eldred, Ken. *The Integrated Life: Experience the Powerful Advantage of Integrating Your FAITH and WORK*. Montrose, CO: Manna Ventures, 2010.

4

Work as Worship

WHAT SONG COMES TO mind when you hear these syllables: *pa-rum-pum-pum-pum*? That beat, of course, runs through the Christmas song about the little drummer boy. Okay, he wasn't really at the manger in Bethlehem. But the assumed story that holds this song together can point to an important truth about our daily work, whether paid or unpaid.

The little drummer boy seems to have been invited by the magi to come with them to see the baby King. They tell the young boy that, to honor this newborn, they are bringing fine gifts to put before the infant. But the little snare drummer, like the baby, is also a poor boy. He has no gift suitable to give to a King.

But then, when he sees the baby, a fresh idea takes hold. He asks the baby's mother if he should play for the baby on his drum. Mary nods her approval. So the boy proceeds to play for him on his little drum.

The boy wants to come with an offering to worship the King. But he has nothing to bring except his drum and his ability to play it. And as he does so, the boy notices that the baby is smiling at him. What relief! His worship-offering has been accepted.

Work as Offering

Have you ever thought of your ordinary, daily work as an offering? As an activity that can be offered in worship God gladly accepts? "Wait!" you may be thinking. "Like texting and driving, worship and work don't mix. Each has its own proper place." Sadly, too many Christians see worship and work that way.

It seems that a great many believers segregate the two in their thinking. Sundays for worship, weekdays for work. A neat way to compartmentalize. But stay with me for a bit. Let's see if we *ought* to keep work and worship in separate drawers.

From the earliest Bible records, worship has involved offerings. Cain and Abel both came to God with offerings. God, we know, accepted only what Abel offered. Abraham trudged up Mt. Moriah, thinking he would have to offer his son Isaac as a sacrifice—but God himself provided the animal for the offering. Tabernacle and temple worship involved a whole range of offerings. The ancient Israelites offered a variety of animals: bulls, rams, lambs, doves, and pigeons. Some offerings included barley, wheat, red wine, yeast, and honey. All need for those old-covenant offerings, though, ended when Jesus offered his own body and blood on the cross. That's why we no longer offer the slaughtered animals.

Does this mean new covenant worship involves no offerings? Hardly. We are still to bring offerings to God—but not all those brought to the tabernacle or temple. Our offerings don't atone for our sins. Instead, they spring from gratitude for the one-time sacrifice Jesus made for them. For example, one offering God still wants us to bring is praise. As Hebrews 13:15 tells us, "Let us continually offer to God a sacrifice of praise—the fruit of lips that confess his name."

Worship as Body-Offering

But there's another gratitude-sacrifice we can bring to God—one explicitly connected with worship. Paul wrote to the Christ followers in Rome that as they gazed on God's mercy in Jesus, they were to "offer your bodies as living sacrifices, holy and pleasing to God—this is your spiritual act of worship" (Rom 12:1). What's happening here? This one sentence connects offerings with bodies; connects bodies with sacrifices; and connects bodily sacrifices with spiritual worship.

Have you ever considered your human body as a *worship* instrument?

"Not so fast," someone might object, "bodies are so *physical*. How could they be spiritual? Praise songs and Bible and prayer and church meetings—those are spiritual. Bodies, on the other hand, are just biodegradable dust. They're so mundane, so ordinary. They get dirty, sweat, need baths, get sick, and finally die. Souls and spirits—those are spiritual. They live forever. Aren't *they* what we should be offering to God in worship?"

But wait. When Jesus said, "Destroy this temple, and I will raise it again in three days," what did he mean by "this temple"? "Well," you say, "he meant his own body—the temple of his body. But of course he *could* say that, because he was Jesus—God in the flesh."

True. But what did Paul go on to say about your body? Don't you know, he asks, "that your bodies are temples of the Holy Spirit?" (1 Cor 6:19). So our physical bodies become spiritual instruments because of the One who lives in them—the Holy Spirit. And because these temple-bodies of ours are spiritual instruments, we can offer them to God in spiritual worship.

Work as a Body-Offering

When you get up, get dressed, and begin your day's work, what instrument do you use to do it? Your body—the "house" that the whole you lives in.

If your work is driving a delivery truck, you use your hands on the steering wheel, your feet on the pedals, and your eyes on the road. Computer programmers use their brains. Singers use their vocal cords. And so on. In other words, this spiritual instrument, this temple of the Holy Spirit, gets involved to accomplish whatever the work may be, whether it's paid or not. Paul urged the

Roman believers to involve their bodies as spiritual vehicles: "So use your whole body as an instrument to do what is right for the glory of God" (Rom 6:13, NLT).

When Eugene Peterson came to Romans 12:1 in *The Message*, here's how he put it: "So here's what I want you to do, God helping you: Take your everyday, ordinary life—your sleeping, eating, going-to-work, and walking-around life—and place it before God as an offering."

Did you catch that reference to work in there? You are to place your "going-to-work . . . life . . . before God as an offering." Yes—one's work life. Work done by the spiritual instrument of the body, the work itself, can be offered to God as an acceptable act of spiritual worship. This is not some radical new idea. Centuries ago, Martin Luther said, "Seemingly secular works are a worship of God and an obedience well pleasing to God."[1]

A Hebrew Word for Work and Worship

Or go back much, much further in history for a look at a surprising word. In the Old Testament, the Hebrew term *avad* is sometimes translated as "worship." For example, at the burning bush God told Moses, "when you have brought the people out of Egypt, you will worship God on this mountain" (Exod 3:12). That English word "worship" translates *avad.*

Now for the surprise. In the fourth of the Ten Commandments, God said, "Six days you shall labor and do all your work" (Exod 20:9). Here, the word "work" translates from *avad.* The same word that means "worship" also means "work."

What links worship and work so closely that the same word can describe both? Deuteronomy 6:13 makes the connection: "Fear the Lord your God, serve him only." The word "serve" in this verse also translates *avad.* In worship, we serve God. In work, we serve God. Do you recall what Paul told the Christian slaves in

1. Morse, "When I Grow Up, I Want to Be . . ."

Colossae about their work? He said, "It is the Lord Christ you are serving" (Col 3:24).

Kamalini Kumar, a nurse, says, "Nursing is my profession, my daily work. But it is also an important way I worship God. For me, work and worship have become like two blades of a scissors; one is useless without the other. I see now that work is a ministry performed before God."[2]

The First Workplace Offerings

Cain and Abel made the first "offerings" we read about in the Bible. Both men offered something from their work. Cain, the farmer, offered what grew from his plot of ground. Abel, the shepherd, offered part of an animal from his flock. So each man offered that which stood for his work. God accepted only one offering. In the letter to the Hebrews, we learn why. Abel made his God-pleasing workplace offering "by faith" (Heb 11:4). Apparently Cain did not, because "without faith, it is impossible to please God" (Heb 11:6).

Our job descriptions define us as accountants, project managers, installers, or what have you. Those are useful as role descriptions. But they do not tell us who we are. Among other biblical terms that reveal our identity is that word "priest." For Christians today, it takes faith to see ourselves doing our work as *priests*.

What do priests do? For old covenant priests, a large part of their work involved making offerings. For new covenant priests, work makes up one of our major offerings. "Whatever you do," Paul instructed the Corinthian Christians, "do it all for the glory of God" (1 Cor 10:31). That "whatever" wraps in everything, including our work. We are to offer, submit, donate our work to God as worship.

"What Is That in Your Hand?"

The little drummer boy saw his drum-playing as worth little compared with the fine gifts of the magi. In a similar way, you may

2. Kumar, "Work as Worship."

have considered so-called "secular" work unfit to offer to Jesus, the King. At the burning bush, Moses did not think he could do the work God was asking him to do—the task of delivering the Israelites from their Egyptian slave masters.

And so God said to him, "What is that in your hand?" Moses knew it was nothing but an ordinary staff. God told him to throw it to the ground. He did, and it became a snake. God then told Moses to take the creature by its tail. When Moses did so, it turned back into a staff.

What is that in *your* hands? What work has God given *you* to do? As you do your work for God's glory, you turn it into a worship offering. As Matthew Kaemingk and Cory B. Willson say in *Work and Worship: Reconnecting Our Labor and Liturgy*, "Gathered worship in the sanctuary must become scattered worship in the streets."[3]

Work as "scattered worship in the streets" has its God-given limits. In Ecclesiastes, the Teacher wrote that "There is a time for everything" (Eccl 3:1). He followed this with a list of opposites, saying there is a time for each corresponding activity on the other end of the scale. He could have added this: *There is a time to work and a time to rest.*

Discussion

1. Your work involves what members of your body?
2. What do you see as the most difficult-to-overcome barriers to offering your daily work as worship?
3. How do you believe these barriers can best be addressed and surmounted?

For more: Chapter 10 of Peabody, Larry. *Job-Shadowing Daniel: Walking the Talk at Work*. Denver: Outskirts, 2010.

3. Kaemingk and Willson, *Work and Worship*, 241.

5

Let's Pause

"I HAVE A PROBLEM," says the main character in a RightNow Media video. "I just can't stop working." The video ends as he says to his support group, "My name is Frank, and I'm a workaholic."[1]

Which do you find easier—to keep on working or to lay your work aside? We've all heard about "workaholics." But do you know who originated that word? Wayne Oates, a psychologist and pastoral counselor, came up with the term back in 1971. He defined "workaholism" as "the compulsion or the uncontrollable need to work incessantly."[2]

From what many people say, we might think it's easier to avoid work than to stay at it. One internet blogger wrote, "I hate working. Plain and simple." Another admitted, "I have hated any sort of work since I was old enough to have chores growing up as a kid."[3] Clearly, some are allergic to work.

Not so with others. Someone named Sarah posted this online: "Last week I wasn't feeling super. I couldn't explain exactly what was wrong. I wasn't sick-sick. I was just . . . exhausted. I decided I

1. RightNow Media, "Workaholic."
2. Oates, *Confessions of a Workaholic*, 3.
4. Green, "I Hate Work, All of It, with a Passion."

needed to give myself a bit of a break. And, right on cue, my mind went: . . . There's so much work to do. Taking the afternoon off would actually be *more* stressful."[4]

The inability to put work on hold, it seems, is not just a product of Western culture. A report from ChinaDaily.com says some 600,000 Chinese per year die from overwork.[5]

God's Guardrail against Overwork

The God who created us to work also knows we can become addicted and enslaved to our work. So he built a guardrail around it. The Old Testament gives us two versions of the Ten Commandments—one in Exodus and the other in Deuteronomy. In each, the order of the commandments is exactly the same. And in each the fourth commandment deals with keeping the Sabbath—the command to rest.

But look at the contrast between the space given to rest and that given to work. In the NIV translation, the command to work takes just ten words in both Exodus and Deuteronomy. However, the command to rest gets eighty-seven words in Exodus and ninety-eight words in Deuteronomy. Ten words for work versus eighty-seven and ninety-eight for rest. It appears, then, that God, in his wisdom, has to lay out on our need to rest in far more detail than our need to work.

First Reason to Stop Working

But let's dig a little deeper. Have you ever noticed that the Exodus account gives one reason for resting, while the Deuteronomy version gives another? In Exodus, the reason given for resting reaches back to the Genesis story of creation. Why work six days, then rest? "For in six days the Lord made the heavens and the earth, the

4. Sarah, "Why Is It So Hard to Give Yourself Permission to Rest?"
5. CRIEnglish.com, "600,000 Chinese Die from Overworking Each Year."

sea, and all that is in them, but he rested on the seventh day" (Exod 31:17). God worked, so we work. God rested, so we rest.

In other words, the Exodus reason for resting is rooted in the fact that we were made in the image of God. By working six days and resting one day we reflect the God who made us in his likeness. In creation, God set up a rhythm—like a drumbeat: *work-work-work-work-work-work—rest; work-work-work-work-work-work—rest.* That rhythm, because it originated in God, is built right into the core of who we, his image-bearers, are and how we best arrange our lives.

Second Reason to Stop Working

But the reason given for resting changes in the Deuteronomy account of the Ten Commandments. Here's the second reason to rest: "Remember that you were slaves in Egypt and that the Lord your God brought you out of there with a mighty hand and an outstretched arm. Therefore the Lord your God has commanded you to observe the Sabbath day" (Deut 5:15).

Back in the Garden of Eden, work for those human beings had been delightful. No weeds to pull. No getting stabbed with the spike of a thorn or thistle. No sweaty foreheads. But by the time of Moses, work for the Israelites had plunged into the territory of a nightmare. It had now become slave labor. As *The Message* paraphrase puts it, the Egyptians "made them miserable with hard labor—making bricks and mortar and back-breaking work in the fields. They piled on the work, crushing them under the cruel workload" (Exod 1:14).

But God intervened. Through a series of miraculous plagues, he unfastened the Israelites from their slave work. So the Deuteronomy reason for resting on the Sabbath is rooted in God's act of setting them free from the endless drudgery of the work they had known in Egypt.

God has given us two reasons for resting. One, because we are made in the image of the God who rested, that *work-work-work-work-work-work—rest* rhythm is part of our makeup. We ignore that rhythm at the risk of our own physical, emotional, and spiritual health. Two, because God freed his people from slave labor, we also have the God-given freedom to take a day completely unhitched from any obligation to work.

Abraham Joshua Heschel, the Jewish rabbi and theologian, describes the Sabbath as part of "the architecture of time." He wrote:

> To set apart one day a week for freedom, a day on which we would not use the instruments which have been so easily turned into weapons of destruction, a day for being with ourselves, a day of detachment from the vulgar, of independence of external obligations, a day on which we stop worshipping the idols of technical civilization, a day on which we use no money, a day of armistice in the economic struggle with our fellow men and the forces of nature—is there any institution that holds out a greater hope for man's progress than the Sabbath?[6]

The Overwork Obsession

Sadly, many of us today ignore the work-rest rhythm we were made for and act as if we were slaves to our work. The book *Fatigue in Modern Society* includes a chapter by André Sarradon in which he says: "If it is difficult to make someone work who does not want to, it is even more difficult to hinder someone from working who wants to, who is obsessed by his activity."[7] But we need to ask: what lies behind this mania for overworking? What makes overworking so tempting?

Drivenness may stem from any number of needs—often the fear of poverty. Many overwork in an effort to guarantee economic safety in the future. Countless articles and ads fan this fear that unless we work extra-hard today, we'll run out of money tomorrow. Here's the fear-inducing headline from a well-known investment magazine: "15 Reasons You'll Go Broke in Retirement."

6. Borneman, "Justice of Sabbath."

7. Tournier. *Fatigue in Modern Society*, 38.

Sometimes the need for significance drives us to draw our identity from our work. Martin Lloyd-Jones, a medical doctor who became a pastor in London, said, "whole cemeteries could be filled with the sad tombstone: 'Born a man, died a doctor.'"[8]

A military general, after retirement, became president of a railroad, yet still insisted that people call him "General." But if we define ourselves by the work we do, who are we when we can no longer work?

Overdoing It—Even in Church Work

Workaholism bites not only those in so-called "secular" occupations but also those in church jobs. Jon Mark Comer, a pastor in Portland, Oregon, admits in his book, *Garden City*, "the reality is I'm a workaholic."[9] At twenty-three, he began planting a church. It took off like a bottle rocket. Conversions. Spiritually transformed lives. And the adrenaline began pumping through the body of this young church planter. Listen to how he, looking back, describes the experience:

> The first year was exhausting but exhilarating. I had never been a part of anything like it. The second year was exhausting but good. The third year was exhausting. That's it. Just exhausting. By the fourth year, I was dying—twenty-seven and on the edge of a nervous breakdown. Stressed out. At the doctor, sick all the time. On edge with my wife. Mad at the world.[10]

Only later was Comer able to diagnose his disease: "I, like a lot of people, was erecting my own Babel, looking to my job for my identity and self-worth." Thankfully, Comer recognized what was happening. In *Garden City*, he describes how he and his family came to establish the practice of Sabbath-rest. He says:

8. Lapp, "Born a Man, Died __________."
9. Comer, *Garden City*, 184.
10. Comer, *Garden City*, 183–84.

> Sabbath isn't just a pause button—it's a full, complete, total system restart. We power down, cool off, let the fan wind down, and then reboot. Sabbath is a chance to take a long, hard look at our lives and to retune them to the right key. To make sure that our life is shaped around what really matters, and then we see stuff in our life that is out of whack. Then we turn to Jesus, and he comes and does his healing Sabbath work.[11]

Workaholism's Real Name

Desperation to find significance and security—or any other unmet needs in our lives—can shift us into work overdrive. What is it when we look to our work instead of God to meet our needs? Let's have the courage to call it by its real name: *idolatry*. Obsessive workaholism turns work into an idol. As Tim Keller explains, setting up idols in our hearts "means imagining and trusting anything to deliver the control, security, significance, satisfaction, and beauty that only the real God can give. It means turning a good thing into an ultimate thing."[12]

Jesus, the risen Lord of the Sabbath, offers us rest. He promises to give us soul rest. Soul rest is not simply a surface rest from activity, but a much deeper rest from anxiety. The good news from Jesus is that significance and security come to us through faith as grace-gifts, not as pay-back for our performance. Relax!

Rest comes easier if you know God has summoned you to what you are doing. But far too many Christians have lived under the uneasy cloud of thinking the only work that really counts with God is "full-time Christian service." That cloud is dark and heavy with rain. It leads us to fill our weekends with hard work in church meetings, in church programs, and on church committees. After all, if our work during the week is not spiritually significant, we are driven to make up for it on Saturdays and Sundays.

11. Comer, *Garden City*, 233.
12. Keller and Alsdorf, *Every Good Endeavor*, 131–32.

The good and relaxing news is that God calls all Christ followers. He sends this one to work in a sales office, that one to work as an attorney, another to work as a farmer, and yet another to work in government. Knowing that your work through the week has been "full-time service" for God, you can then truly relax on your day of rest.

Discussion

1. Respond to this question near the beginning of this chapter: "Which do you find easier—to keep on working or to lay your work aside?" Explain your answer.
2. What factors conspire to press us into overworking?
3. What steps can you take to guard against making your work into an idol?

For more: Chapters 8–10 of Comer, John Mark. *Garden City*. Grand Rapids, MI: Zondervan, 2015.

6

Manage God's Earth

How long could a Cocker Spaniel hold a job? Can sparrows grow food for your table? Would you ask a salmon to build a bridge? No, no, and no. Only human beings have careers, plant and harvest crops, and span rivers with bridges. That's no accident. One major reason God made us different from the animals was so that we can care for his earthly real estate as his property managers.

If you appoint someone to manage your property, you'd better make certain they're qualified. Several years ago, the owners of a house across the street from ours moved more than two thousand miles away. Rather than selling their home, they decided to rent it out and hire a property manager.

We shook our heads as a succession of renters came and went. Tenant screening went from bad to worse. In time, the man in one renter household, just out of prison, began selling drugs out of the home. Inside and out, the house began to deteriorate; the front porch steps sagged. A toilet overflowed and soaked the carpet. Why the downhill slide? Poor decisions and irresponsibility on the part of the property manager.

Caretakers for Planet Earth

God's activity in creation provided him with a vast earthly estate. It included lands, rivers and bodies of water, an atmosphere, plants, and animals of all kinds. He looked it all over and pronounced it good. But the whole project needed caretakers. So God consulted within himself and said:

"Let us make human beings in our image, make them reflecting our nature So they can be responsible for the fish in the sea, the birds in the air, the cattle, And, yes, Earth itself, and every animal that moves on the face of Earth" (Gen 1:26, MSG).

After creating suitable property managers, he left them his job description: "Prosper! Reproduce! Fill Earth! Take charge! Be responsible for fish in the sea and birds in the air, for every living thing that moves on the face of Earth" (Gen 1:28, MSG).

Genesis spells out some of what God meant when he told us to govern or rule the earth. He placed Adam in the Garden of Eden "to work it and take care of it" (Gen 2:15). There it is! We rule the earth through our work. Planting, watering, cultivating, harvesting. God's Garden wasn't going to take care of itself. As Genesis 2:5 explains, God even held back on the growth of vegetation, because "there was no one to work the ground." Work—there's that word again.

With Noah, God extends and expands the human assignment to rule the earth. In Genesis 9:1, God tells Noah and his sons, "Be fruitful and increase in number and fill the earth." God repeats this command and adds to it in verse 7: "As for you, be fruitful and increase in number; multiply on the earth and increase upon it."

In his *Genesis* commentary, Walter Brueggemann says,

> Post-flood humankind is in God's image, responsible for and capable of rule . . . The ruling human is entrusted with a fresh rule (9:1–7). In Genesis 1:26, the human creature was to rule over fish, birds, and animals. This meant to bring the other creatures to fullness. But now the New Being is to preside over humankind in order to enhance, celebrate, and dignify it.[1]

1. Brueggemann, *Genesis*, 83.

The "Masks of God"

The Psalmist says it is God who "gives food to every creature" (Ps 136:25). But how does God do that? Think of your breakfast this morning. Did God rain manna down from heaven? Will he bring you quail for dinner? He has fed people in those ways in the past—and he still could. But he chooses to involve us. He does his work of feeding people around the world through the hard work of their fellow human beings. The work of farmers. Harvesters. Truck drivers. Warehouse operators. Grocery clerks. And cooks.

In his "Exposition of Psalm 147," Martin Luther wrote:

> God could easily give you grain and fruit without your plowing and planting. But He does not want to do so . . . What else is all our work to God—whether in the fields, in the garden, in the city, in the house, in war, or in government—but just such a child's performance, by which He wants to give His gifts in the fields, at home, and everywhere else? These are the masks of God, behind which He wants to remain concealed and do all things.[2]

Have you ever thought of your work as a "mask" of God? From all everyone in world can see, the work of bakers keeps us supplied with bread, the work of carpenters with tables, and the work of pilots with safe landings. But behind the scenes, behind the "masks," stands God who does these and so many other earth-care responsibilities through human beings made in his likeness.

So by working each of us is stepping up to our responsibility to serve as God's agent by providing for and sustaining life on planet Earth.

God's Gearmaker

Sometimes we simply do not see how vital certain mundane work really is—how it contributes to maintaining an environment in which life in God's world can thrive. For example, how can

2. Greear, "Martin Luther on the 'Masks of God.'"

something as ordinary as a toothed gear make it possible for life on planet earth to continue?

A friend of mine, Dave Hataj, owns and operates a machine shop in Wisconsin. Edgerton Gear makes tiny gears and supersized ones up to five feet in diameter. They create gears out of wear-resistant nylon and special steels. How does my friend's work as a gear-maker carry out the role of property manager over God's world? How on earth does his work sustain plants, animals, and people?

Let's explore that question by asking by thinking back to breakfast again. What did you eat this morning? Granola? How did those crunchy chunks reach your bowl? Someone probably drove in a car to the store to buy it. How many gears are in a car? How many in the conveyor belt at the checkout stand? How many in the truck that delivered the granola to the store?

Think too about the gear-filled farm tractors, irrigation systems, and harvesting machines involved in producing the grain. Did you eat your granola with milk? Feeding cows takes crop-harvesting machines, hay balers, and conveyor belts—none of which could run without gears. The pumps in milking machines depend on gears. No gears, no milk.

My friend also sustains some twenty-five employees on his payroll, providing them with the income they need to provide granola and milk for their families. Working to produce gears makes it possible for them to pay the mortgage, take family vacations, and share with others in need. In addition, my friend brings high-school students right into his shop, where his machinists, working as mentors, coach them in responsible craftsmanship.

I am writing this as we are nearing the end (we hope!) of the COVID-19 pandemic. Back when all the shutdowns began, my friend Dave thought for sure he would have to lay off most of his crew. Much to his surprise, he discovered that gear-makers turned out to be essential workers. Why? Because suddenly buyers were rushing out to buy toilet paper. So Edgerton Gear was swamped with orders from toilet-paper manufacturers needing replacement gears.

Even these few examples leave no doubt: the work of making gears benefits the living inhabitants of God's earth. Gear-making—another "mask" behind which God provides for his world. You may read Dave Hataj's story in his book, *Good Work: How Blue Collar Business Can Change Lives, Communities, and the World.*

Managing God's Classroom Property

During my first year of college, I took a janitorial job. My territory—the third floor of a junior high school (something later known as middle school). For each room, the job description was what you would expect. Move the desks to sweep the floor. Put the desks back into straight ranks. Dust the desks. Clean the chalkboard. And empty the wastebaskets.

Unless I had done my work, those classrooms would have turned into such chaotic messes that faculty would have refused to teach there, and parents would have pulled their kids out of school. After my orientation, no one told me what to do or when to do it. In other words, when it came to the care of floor 3 in that school, I had the rule over it. I was shepherd-king, the cleanup czar in those rooms.

As part of God's earth, those classrooms belonged to him. I ruled over them by working as his property manager, seeking to see that his will was done in that part of his earth as it is in heaven.

Let me suggest a game you can play with family members or friends. Search online for help-wanted ads—you know, the kind that list a job title and a bit of information about what the work will involve. Then see how well you and those with you can describe how the person who fills that job will be doing their share in tending God's earth. To get you started, I've included five job titles I just found advertised online:

Veterinary Front Office Receptionist. In addition to tasks like answering the telephone and billing clients, a veterinary's receptionist may help remove animals from cages, weigh them, and carry them to the examination room. How does this work carry out God's will? We know that God delegated to humans the care for "every living creature that moves on the ground" (Gen 1:28). God cares about his earthly animals.

Housekeeper / House Cleaner. The wellbeing of those in a home partly depends on it being clean and uncluttered. Unsanitary countertops can harbor dangerous bacteria. Floors covered with carelessly tossed clothing and objects become tripping hazards. The house cleaner is serving God's interest in protecting the lives of people—an interest reflected in this verse: "When you build a new house, you must build a railing around the edge of its flat roof. That way you will not be considered guilty of murder if someone falls from the roof" (Deut 22:8, NLT).

Retail Stocking Associate. Someone in this position will make certain that products in this hardware store are available and accessible to buyers. Many of the items in the inventory are essential for life in the twenty-first century to flourish—hammers, chisels, pipe wrenches, and on and on. A stock associate helps to carry out God's will that his earth be filled with humans properly provided for. God told his people living in Babylon to "build houses and settle down; plant gardens and eat what they produce" (Jer 29:5). If Jesus were to operate his construction business today, he might well depend on the work of a retail stocking associate.

Fingerprint Technician. In its present condition, God's earth includes those who steal from, injure, abuse, and kill people made in God's image. A fingerprint technician serves the purposes of God by assisting "God's servants [who are his] agents of wrath to bring punishment on the wrongdoer" (Rom 13:4).

Universal Banker. This role includes opening and servicing all kinds of savings and deposit accounts. If human life on earth is to flourish, it requires a functioning economy (on this, see comments by Lester DeKoster in chapter 2 of *Work: The Meaning of Your Life*). Through savings and deposit accounts flow the funds that fuel such life-sustaining economic activity—and empowering people in countless ways to carry out God's will on earth as it is done in heaven.

The King of creation has credentialed you to serve him as a "governor" over this or that part of his earth. No matter what the work—paid or not—it involves serving as God's property manager who expresses love for him and for others through work. By scattering his property managers all around the world, Jesus has made a way for his rulership extend even into the remotest corners of the globe.

Discussion

1. Martin Luther called the varieties of human work the "masks of God." Is that a helpful analogy for you? Why or why not?
2. How does your work contribute something to the grand task of managing God's earthly real estate?
3. Visualize what would happen if all garbage collectors in your state went on strike. What lessons can you take from that imagined picture?

For more: Chapter 1 of Van Duzer, Jeff. *Why Business Matters to God (And What Still Needs to Be Fixed)*. Downers Grove, IL: InterVarsity, 2010.

7

Your Share

PARIS. THE RENOWNED CITY of love. The legendary city of lights. But for those living there, recent events might have suggested a different nickname. On February 4, 2020, sanitation workers went on strike to protest the pension reforms proposed by French President Emmanuel Macron. Thousands of tons of garbage soon piled up. Some residents even began dumping their own trash in the streets.

"What's worrying," said one city-dweller, "is seeing little rats running into the streets far more easily. It's an open bar." Another complained, "It's ugly. It's unhealthy."[1] In the world's pecking order of desirable jobs, collecting garbage ranks near the bottom. And yet, when sanitation workers stop doing their work, not only the air but life itself begins to stink.

Each of the billions of people in the world's labor force working in a legitimate job is doing their own small part in helping life on God's earth to flourish. In the beginning, God gave his reason for creating human beings: so that they would rule over, take responsibility for, life on his earth (Gen 1:26).

1. Biffot-Lacout, "'Open Bar' for Rats as Paris Pension Strikes Hit Waste Collection."

God Delights in His Earth

In *The Divine Conspiracy*, Dallas Willard tells of a visit to South Africa, where he walked along an ocean beach that caused him to stand "in stunned silence . . . I saw space and light and texture and color and power . . . that seemed hardly of this earth."

Then it hit Willard:

> God sees this all the time . . . It is perhaps strange to say, but suddenly I was extremely happy for God and thought I had some sense of what an infinitely joyous consciousness he is and of what it might have meant for him to look at his creation and find it "very good."[2]

God prizes and stands up for his "very good" creation. The twenty-four elders in John's vision of heaven thank God that in his wrath he will destroy "those who destroy the earth" (Rev 11:18). Just as he freed the ancient Israelites from their Egyptian slavemasters, God will come to the rescue of his whole creation, setting it free (Rom 8:21).

A Persistent Lie

According to Genesis, God's stated reason for creating us is that we might see to it that life on his earth flourishes. Doesn't this provide us with still another good reason for getting up and going to work? Having this responsibility entrusted to us dignifies who we are. Yet the unbiblical idea still persists among Christians—that regular (non-church) work doesn't matter that much to God, even if that work helps to maintain the planet and its life.

A friend once told me that two years earlier his brother and sister-in-law had begun making plans to quit their jobs. I asked why, and my friend explained. The brother worked in a lumber company as a building-supply salesman. His wife, employed by a government agency, taught life skills to those with disabilities.

2. Willard, *Divine Conspiracy*, 73.

But, as they put it, they wanted to "do something for God." So they announced that they intended to quit their jobs, sell their house, buy a motorhome, and travel across the United States with their three children ministering to people in RV parks.

"But aren't you serving God and people where you work now?" my friend asked. "No," they said, "our jobs are not like '*real* ministries.'" My friend kept up his challenge: "Who will pay your way? Are you going to ask others who earn money from 'non-ministry' jobs to give you funds so that you may do 'ministry?'" His persistent questions paid off. As it turned out, they decided to abandon their RV plans.

I asked my friend why they had not seen regular work as ministry. He said his sister-in-law had grown up in a church tradition with heavy emphasis on short-term missions but no emphasis on God's purposes in the work most people do over the long term. That lack of teaching about how our daily work carries out God's will on earth produces Christians who see little or no faith-related reason to get up and go to work in a so-called "secular" job.

Will This Earth Be Trashed?

But the problem is not always the *absence* of teaching. Sometimes it is the *presence* of misleading teaching. From what I was taught, I grew up with the idea that the present earth will be burned up, trashed. Then God will start all over again, from scratch, and create another earth, a completely different one. This teaching was inspired largely by 2 Peter 3:10, which says, "The heavens will disappear with a roar; the elements will be destroyed by fire, and the earth and everything done in it will be laid bare." Peter goes on to say, "everything will be destroyed in this way."

It sure looks as if this present earth is just a throwaway, like a used paper plate after a picnic. If true, that kind of teaching makes it difficult to get motivated to spend any time caring for earth and its concerns. But wait. Glance back at the context—at what Peter says in verse 6. Speaking of Noah and the great flood, he says, "By these waters also the world of that time was deluged and destroyed."

Of course we know that Noah's world was not "destroyed" in the sense that it ceased to exist. In Genesis 7:20, the water "covered the mountains," and when the water receded, "the tops of the mountains became visible" (Gen 8:5). The mountains before and after the flood were the same mountains. So the earth was "destroyed" in the sense that the evil in it was wiped out. This and other Scriptures help us to see that the 2 Peter passage tells us the coming fire will burn all the evil out of the earth, just as fire purges iron ore of its impurities.

Romans 8:21, mentioned earlier, promises that "the creation itself will be liberated from its bondage to decay and brought into the freedom and glory of the children of God." Liberated. Annihilation would leave nothing to be liberated. In the beginning, God repeatedly said his earthly creation was "good." Although it suffers under the plague of sin, the earth has not lost its goodness. So God intends to rescue his good world from all that holds it captive, setting it free to be a renewed earth.

Even in its present unliberated form, God values the earth—including its plants, animals, and people. "The Lord has established his throne in heaven, and his kingdom rules over all" (Ps 103:19). And "he who fashioned and made the earth, he founded it; he did not create it to be empty, but formed it to be inhabited" (Isa 45:18).

Sustaining Life on Planet Earth

Maintaining an earth that can "be inhabited" takes a tremendous amount of labor as we await God's new creation. God is working out his purposes in his earth as it now exists. He is providing a grace period in which people may turn from their sin to his Son. He is purifying his church. And while God is carrying out those purposes, life here must be sustained and maintained.

As we've seen, the planet is currently in temporary bondage to frustration. The world-systems have fallen under the sway of the evil one. But it is still true that "the earth is the Lord's and everything in it" (1 Cor 10:26). This real property still rightly belongs to the One who created it.

Earth now supports nearly eight billion people. Maintaining an environment fit for human life is complicated and demanding. The task breaks down into what seems like an endless variety of occupations. For example, consider our food supply. Eating an apple for lunch seems simple enough. But getting that fruit into your mouth involved the labor of a great many contributors.

- The nursery that provided the seedling trees.
- The farmer who bought land, planted an orchard, and cultivated it for years before it bore any fruit.
- The companies that produced pesticides and fertilizers to keep the tree alive and healthy.
- The county extension agent who helped the farmer understand how to grow apples.
- The hired harvester who pulled the ripe apple from the branch.
- The trucker who hauled it to a warehouse.
- The other truck drivers who delivered it to a grocery store near your home.
- The owner who invested in that grocery outlet.
- The employee who placed the apple on display in the produce department.
- The cashier who put the apple in your carry-out bag.

And after all that, you still paid only fifty cents for the apple!

Just as God created all else by speaking it into existence, he launched our work on earth with his words when he made us: "Let us make man in our image, in our likeness, and let them rule over . . . all the earth" (Gen 1:26). From that beginning, earthwork—like the human population—has expanded immensely. Earthwork includes both paid and unpaid work. In 2021, the civilian labor force alone included roughly 160 million paid jobs in the United States. The amount and value of unpaid work cannot be calculated.

So whatever your earthwork, you can do it as a service lovingly offered to God. You serve by helping to maintain his earth and sustain life on this planet in the here and now. Your work itself has value both to God and to earth's inhabitants.

God's Property Managers

Imagine you are watching a series of flash cards, each one with a single word on it. You see each card for less than a second. The final word is: **S-T-E-W-A-R-D-S-H-I-P.**

Quick—say your first thought. What does that word mean?

Dennis Bakke recognizes what it suggests to many Christians:

> Unfortunately, "stewardship" is a word that the church usually associates with charitable giving and tithing. It has come to refer to the small amount of money people give away, rather than the money they make and the talents they use to celebrate God in their daily lives.[3]

Words—like sweaters in a washing machine—can shrink. Our church traditions have "smallified" the term "stewardship." In his little book, *Work: The Meaning of Your Life*, Lester DeKoster notes that "churches usually limit their concept of how we serve God ('stewardship') to formally religious activities."[4]

DeKoster points out that our word "stewardship" came to us via the Greek word *oikonomia*. If you say that ancient word out loud—*oy-koh-no-meeya*—it sounds very much like our word for it in English. "*Economics*," says DeKoster, speaks of "the management of things in the world. Good stewardship is good management of things in the world." He continues:

> Economics is the social system through which individuals organize and exchange their work and its fruits. All economic activity—such as owning property, buying and

3. Bakke, *Joy at Work*, 265.
4. DeKoster, *Work: The Meaning of Your Life*, 65.

> selling, employment, contracts, finance and investment, business and entrepreneurship—is ultimately grounded in people's work.[5]

In the church world, we typically use "stewardship" and "steward" as nouns. But dictionaries also list "steward" as a verb. As an action word, "to steward" means to manage the property of someone else in a way that serves the owner's purposes.

Your job—whatever it may be—belongs to God. As one of the "things in the world" (God's world), your job is his property. You don't own it. Instead, you have received the temporary right to use it to carry out God's purposes in that particular area.

To steward your job, you'll need to stay in touch with God to discover all of his aims in that specific area of his property. The Bible is full of God's word on work. But the sacred-secular divide has made it difficult to connect the biblical dots between so-called "secular work" and God's purposes for life on earth. Yes, it's easy to see God's hand in the work of a pastor or missionary. But what about the work of plumbers? Of graphic artists? Of commercial pilots?

Maintaining life here on God's earth might be compared with providing for those aboard the International Space Station (ISS). Sustaining human life on board the ISS takes some doing. NASA calls the challenge of building and maintaining the space base a very complex task. Spacecraft missions must continually replenish the supply of food and water for the ISS crew—a payload of more than a metric ton in one recent visit. Even the repair of a space toilet requires expertise and effort.

Keeping life livable on planet Earth—God's "space station"—also requires immense and constant maintenance. God himself put the raw materials on board: soil, water, air, animal life, vegetation, and so on. But he assigned to human beings a large role in maintaining this orbiting space station. Think of your work role as earthwork. God's earthwork. And let the truth of that motivate you to go back to work tomorrow.

5. DeKoster, *Work: The Meaning of Your Life*, 65–66.

Discussion

1. Finish this sentence: God created us human beings to . . .
2. If reading this chapter changed your idea of "stewardship," describe the shift in your thinking.
3. What would life on earth miss if no one in the world did the kind of work you do?

For more: Chapter 15 of Miller, Darrow L. *LifeWork: A Biblical Theology for What You Do Every Day*. Seattle: YWAM, 2009.

8

The Light Shines

IN WHAT WAY ARE we Christians just like Jesus?

A cheeky, irreverent question, someone might say. But what if Jesus made that point? Speaking of himself, Jesus said: "I am the light of the world." And on another occasion, speaking to his disciples, he said, "You are the light of the world." In other words, God has given us—the followers of Jesus—a role identical to one of Jesus' own roles. A world-lighting role.

Lighting Up Dark Caves

A little light goes a long way. When I was thirteen, my family and I trekked in a '51 Plymouth from the State of Washington to Ohio. We made this trip just before the US built interstate freeways. Along the way, our dad acquired a fascination with caves. So when the Montana road signs announced the Lewis and Clark Caverns just ahead, Dad couldn't resist.

He paid the entrance fee for all six of us. The guide led us deep into the earth. Finally, our tour group paused in a massive chamber with stalactites hanging like icicles from the ceiling and stalagmites sprouting from the floor like asparagus. Then the guide announced he would turn off the lights. Suddenly, a suffocating darkness engulfed us. I couldn't even see my hand three inches from my eyes.

After letting the experience with inky blackness sink in, the guard struck a match. Suddenly, darkness no longer ruled the cave. No, there was not enough light to read by. But at least we could walk without banging our heads or skinning our elbows on those stalactites and stalagmites.

Like that cavern, your workplace is one of spiritual darkness. Paul spoke of "this dark world" (Eph 6:12). The world of work forms a major part of this dark world. How major? Worldwide, almost half the population of our planet make up the world's workforce.

Sometimes workplace darkness is cleverly camouflaged, sometimes it's blatant—but it's always present. It lurks behind polite-but-false smiles and political correctness. Behind the belittling remarks of coworkers. Behind apathy. Disengagement. Discrimination. Envy. Favoritism. Laziness. Gossip. Greed. Arrogance. Deception. Prejudice. Selfish ambition. Sexual harassment. Cutthroat rivalry. Long-held grudges. Theft. Unforgiveness. Bitterness. Bullying. Insubordination. Darkness runs deep in workplace caves.

Dark Places—Our Assignment

Too often Christians see workplace darkness as a reason to escape from so-called "secular" work. A former solder said, "I soon found that the military was really no place for a Christian. Daily my ears were assaulted with profane and obscene language." Church friends advised a graphic designer that he "should not be involved in three types of jobs: an artist (due to widespread worldly temptation), a politician (because it's 'dirty') or a lawyer (to avoid the lure of wealth)." A blogger warns, "The workplace is no place for a Christian woman. It is too hard to be spiritual there . . . Stay out of the world!"[1]

1. Kohl, "Should a Christian Mother Work outside the Home?"

And yet . . . that dark world with its murky work-caves is the very one into which Jesus sends us. It is not to be avoided; it is our assignment. We are not to escape it in fear but to enter it in faith. Jesus told his Father, "as you sent me into the world, I have sent them into the world." How could this not include the work world?

The darkness there—far from being a reason to leave it—is precisely the reason to penetrate and remain in the world of work. More than anything, those in the dark need light. We Christ followers are the light of the world. Without us, people in the world grope around in the dark, without even so much as the light from a match.

Is it a stretch to think any of us can light up the dark corner of the work world we're in? Jesus calls us the light of the world, but how can that be? And, of course, we can't make it happen on our own. The light we have is "borrowed." Borrowed from Jesus.

As Paul puts it, "For you were once darkness, but now you are light in the Lord" (Eph 5:8). In him, both Jesus and Paul tell us, we may become children of light. Like everything else in the Christian experience, we need to get a grip on this truth through faith.

Work as a Light-Conductor

Okay, so let's say Christian working people really begin to believe they are God's lights in the darkened work world. But how does the light of Christ stream out of them and into that spiritual night? By what means can the light of Christ in them flow out into their work environment? Won't the work culture block or put out the light?

Jesus tells us in Matthew 5:16, "Let your light shine before men, that they may see your good deeds and praise your Father in heaven." In the original Greek, that word "deeds" is literally the word for work. Put that in the workplace context. The light shines, Jesus is saying, through all kinds of good work those around can see.

In that vein, Dorothy Sayers, the British writer and poet, wrote:

> The church's approach to an intelligent carpenter is usually confined to exhorting him not to be drunk and disorderly in his leisure hours, and to come to church on

> Sundays. What the church should be telling him is this: that the very first demand that his religion makes upon him is that he should make good tables . . . No crooked table legs or ill-fitting drawers ever, I dare swear, came out of the carpenter's shop at Nazareth. Nor, if they did, could anyone believe that they were made by the same hand that made heaven and earth.[2]

Martin Luther said: "The Christian shoemaker does his Christian duty not by putting little crosses on the shoes, but by making good shoes, because God is interested in good craftsmanship."[3] Or as Tim Keller explains the responsibility of a Christian pilot: "Land the plane." And land it "so it can take off again."[4]

In her book, *I Came Only for English . . .*, Ruth Kowalczuk tells of an international group who went to Poland in the 1980s and 1990s to teach English:

> We made it clear from the very beginning that our primary and most important Christian witness should be quality teaching . . . The witness of a job well done was very special in those days, because during the decades of communism, people used a rather slapdash manner of work.[5]

Everyday work others can see, like the lens in a lighthouse, transmits the light of Jesus within the worker so that others can see it. No workplace culture can shut out light-conducting work.

Each Job a Lampstand

Imagine yourself working as an accountant, a homemaker, a grocery clerk, an attorney, a barista, or something else. Whatever the job, the position itself—the station you occupy—plays an important part in your light-bearing role. Look again at what Jesus says

2. Sayers, "Why Work?"
3. Goodreads, "Martin Luther."
4. Padilla, "All Work Is God's Work."
5. Kowalczuk, *I Came Only for English*, 57.

about our being the light of the world in Matthew 5. After lighting a lamp, he says, no one buries it under a bowl. "Instead they put it on its stand, and it gives light to everyone in the house" (Matt 5:15).

The work post—the job itself—is that stand, that lampstand. What is the role of a lampstand? It holds the light steady in a strategic spot over a long period of time. I have a lamp beside the chair I like to sit in while I read. The bulb is held firmly in place by a stand—I can count on the light being there, right where I need it.

A job position—however insignificant it may seem as measured by the world's yardstick—is a Christian's lampstand. It keeps the one filling the job in a fixed place among a certain group of people for months and even years. From their stable positions, Jesus' lighted ones shine into the darkness of the particular "caves" they are working in.

In *Every Good Endeavor*, Tim Keller tells of speaking with a woman he had noticed visiting Redeemer Presbyterian Church in New York City. When he asked her how she had come to start attending there, she told him this story.

Shortly after she began working for a TV studio in Manhattan, she made a serious error for which she expected to get fired. To her surprise, her boss told management the fault was his for not training her better. This cost him some standing in the company. Stunned, she thanked her boss profusely. In previous jobs, she had seen others steal the kudos for work she had done. But never in her life had anyone paid the price for her mistake. Why, she wanted to know, had he done what he did?

At first, he tried to brush it off, but she insisted he tell her. Finally he said,

> "I am a Christian. That means among other things that God accepts me because Jesus Christ took the blame for things that I have done wrong. He did that on the cross. That I why I have the desire and sometimes the ability to take the blame for others."
>
> After she took in what he had just said, she asked, "Where do you go to church?"[6]

6. Keller and Alsdorf, *Every Good Endeavor*, 219.

This woman's boss, from his lampstand, was able to shine light into his workplace "cave" by the way he did his supervisory work. And by his action, he himself as well as his employee took further steps on the road to Christlikeness.

Discussion

1. What need for spiritual, moral, or ethical light have you seen where you work?
2. What makes a job position such an ideal "lampstand" in our culture?
3. Why do you think many Christians have drawn back from dark places rather than going into *all* the world as Jesus calls us to do?

For more: Chapter 3 of Peabody, Larry. *Serving Christ in the Workplace: Secular Work Is Full-Time Service.* Peabody, MA: Christian Literature Crusade, 1974.

9

Blessing God's World

"No one should ever work," says Bob Black in "The Abolition of Work." "Work is the source of nearly all the misery in the world. Almost any evil you'd care to name comes from working or from living in a world designed for work. In order to stop suffering, we have to stop working."[1]

Black's statement, "No one should ever work," begs some obvious questions. How did he expect his book to get published if no one worked? Would magic paper for the pages just flutter like manna from the sky? What kind of ink could he have found that no one worked to produce? Without his own work as a writer and that of printers, how would his words have been arranged in a manuscript and bound into a book?

Writing in *Sojourners*, Paul Del Junco seems to agree with Black: "By its very nature, all work is cursed. Work is the direct result of the Fall of Adam and Eve."[2]

As the title of this chapter implies, work blesses the world. But according to Del Junco, "work is cursed." And Black associates

1. Black, "Abolition of Work."
2. Del Junco, "Curse of Work."

work with "evil." Who's right? Is work a curse? Or is it a blessing? Let's begin with some definitions.

- A curse calls for hurtful judgment following a wrong. Curses lead to loss.
- A blessing calls for God's favor freely given. Blessings lead to gain.

In the Bible, "bless" is often used as a verb asking another to speak well about or to praise someone or something. When we ask God to bless others, the verb is also asking for action—that God do something favorable for them. When Ruth, speaking of Boaz, said to her daughter-in-law, Naomi, "The Lord bless him" (Ruth 2:19), she was asking God to show him kindness.

When the action of the "bless" verb reaches its object, the result is the noun, "blessing." A blessing is the favorable contribution or benefit received by a person or a group of people. When God told Abram, "I will bless you . . . and you will be a blessing" (Gen 12:2), he was promising that he would do good for Abram and that, as a result, the blessed Abram would be one who brought about good for others.

The blessing God promised Abram/Abraham would ultimately come through Jesus Christ, his death, resurrection, and ascension. What Jesus did unleashed a whole new band of people equipped with Abraham's power to bless. "Understand, then, that those who have faith are children of Abraham . . . So those who rely on faith are blessed along with Abraham, the man of faith" (Gal 3:7, 9). We Christ followers, as heirs of Abraham's blessing, are given the capacity to bless others.

The One Blessed Becomes One Who Blesses

God blessed Abraham so that he could bless others. Abraham the *blessed one* became Abraham the *one who blessed*. God blesses us with the same goal in mind—that we in turn bless others. God has built this *blessing-that-leads-to-blessing* pattern into his creation. For example:

I grew up on a family farm of thirty acres situated in a desert. How could our acreage, in an area with only 7.5 inches of rainfall a year, keep sugar beets, corn, and other row crops alive in prolonged heat of ninety-plus degrees? The secret, 130 miles away, stood fourteen thousand feet tall: *Mt. Rainier*. Each winter, the sky blanketed the mountain with deep snow. Come summer, melt from the snow ran into the Yakima River and then into the hundred-mile-long Roza Canal. We irrigated our crops with water from that canal. So the sky "blessed" Mt. Rainier with snow, and Mt. Rainier "blessed" our farm with the water from that snow.

If I could pack the message of this chapter into just two words, they would be: "Work blesses." That mini-sentence carries two ideas. First, through their work, God blesses the workers themselves. For those with eyes able to see it, God blesses us even through difficult work or work we would not choose. Second, the God-blessed workers are then able to extend blessings to others through the work they do.

Receiving Blessings through Work

As already noted, Bob Black sees work as "the source of nearly all the misery in the world."[3] But as the examples that follow make clear, God uses work as the channel to dispense a great many blessings.

I experienced one of those blessings early on. Our farm was especially good at growing weeds. At least that's how it seemed to me as the boy who had to keep cutting them out. I remember one especially large outcropping of lamb's quarters (*Chenopodium album*—Why do weeds deserve Latin names?). Eager to have the job over with, I began hacking away with my hoe in the middle of the patch. Dad stopped me, took the hoe, and showed me how it should be done. "Begin at the edge and pull away the weeds you cut," he said, demonstrating how to do so. "If you bury the

3. Black, "Abolition of Work."

still-living weeds under the now-dead ones, they'll hide from your hoe and survive."

Dad's lesson probably took a minute or less, but it has stayed with me for all the decades since. And I have applied the principle to situations far removed from farm life. Basically, I learned to approach any task with the question: Given the project at hand, what should I do first? What action sequence does this task call for?

- *Am I about to sell our home and move?* What step should I lead with?
- *Am I writing a letter asking someone for help?* How should the letter begin to prepare the reader for a response?
- *Am I preparing a meal for guests?* How should I start? What cooking order shall I follow so the various foods will all be ready to serve hot at mealtime?

This basic lesson in strategic thinking came to me as a blessing. And it came to me through work.

The noted theologian Stanley Hauerwas recognizes a blessing that came to him through working: "My father was a better bricklayer than I am a theologian. I am still in too much of a hurry. But if the work I have done in theology is of any use, it is because of what I learned on the job, that is, you can lay only one brick at a time."[4]

In her book *Be a Blessing*, Elizabeth Ellen Ostring writes:

> To work in blessing invokes the important choice factor of attitude, and challenges current notions of reward and incentive . . . The Genesis account notes that unpleasant occupation can be forced upon a person: Joseph had no choice about being sold as a slave, or being sent to prison. But he did have a choice about his attitude, and his choices proved to be a blessing to himself and others.[5]

4. Goodreads, "Stanley Hauerwas."

5. Ostring, *Be a Blessing*, 250.

Examples of blessings coming to us through our work are endless. But, as in the case of Abraham, God blesses us Christians so that we in turn may bless others.

Extending Blessings through Work

The conversation in the restaurant took an unexpected turn. My wife and I were enjoying a noon meal with some Christian friends we've known for years. I'll call them Frank and Rose. Both of them grew up in church and have been heavily involved in church leadership. After the dialog had zigged and zagged through several subjects, Rose began telling us about her disappointment with their adult daughter. Living on some acreage, the daughter is spending her time farming! Her large garden helps feed the children. When she walks outside, goats follow her around!

Rose could not hide her disgust. "If she's going to be just a farmer, why did she earn a doctorate?" I pointed to Rose's lunch. "What are you eating?" I asked. "Chicken," she said, "and a biscuit." "You've also just finished a green salad," I added. Looking across to Frank's plate, I asked her, "And who made it possible for him to order that broccoli?"

Before our meal, we had all thanked God for the food before us. He had blessed us all through the work of food-producing farmers. But to Rose, those farmers seemed commonplace. She could eat her food without appreciating them, because the work they did had no status in her value system.

Have you ever thought of all the "invisible" people whose work blessed Jesus and, as a result, continues to bless us today? In his life and ministry here on earth, Jesus relied on products that working people had made. In doing much of what he did, Jesus counted on what people working with their hands had produced. This began right at his birth and continued until his death.

Cloth Weavers

Luke tells us that when Jesus was born, Mary "wrapped him in cloths and placed him in a manger" (Luke 2:7). Those strips of cloth did not just miraculously appear for the birth event. Someone had woven them beforehand. And the manger? Many think it would have been carved from stone. If so, long hours of work had gone into shaping it into a trough that would hold food for animals. A weaver and stonemason blessed the baby Jesus through their work.

Synagogue Builders

During his ministry, Jesus taught people in various venues. Sometimes he talked to those in synagogues. It was in the Capernaum synagogue that Jesus spoke about eating his flesh and drinking his blood—a statement that led many to stop following him. A fourth-century synagogue, still in Capernaum, stands on the first-century foundation of the synagogue that Jesus undoubtedly taught in. The foundation was made of black basalt stone. The project probably was constructed by a crew of builders who, through their work, blessed Jesus by providing a place for him to teach.

Perfumers

While Jesus was sharing a meal in a home in Bethany, Lazarus and Martha's sister Mary came to him with "about a pint of pure nard, an expensive perfume" (John 12:3). Much to the disgust of Judas, she poured the whole pint of perfume on Jesus. The fragrant nard, not native to Israel, had undoubtedly come from East India—making it a costly substance. But before it reached Mary's hands, it had to be formulated by a perfumer and transported, perhaps by traders, to where she could purchase it.

Scroll Makers

Shortly after being tempted by the devil, Jesus went on the Sabbath into the synagogue in his hometown of Nazareth. Someone handed him a scroll and he began reading from Isaiah. We easily pass quickly over that word "scroll" without realizing the skilled work it took to make one.

After harvesters had cut papyrus, the scroll-maker split thin but wide sheets from each triangular stalk. Next, these sheets were flattened on a wet board, pounded to squeeze out surplus water, and dried under the sun. Using shells or ivory, the worker leveled out rough areas to make a smooth writing surface. Glue made from flour, water, and vinegar usually held twenty sheets together. When these were rolled, they formed a regular scroll. More work followed when scribes painstakingly copied Isaiah's words onto the scroll.

Shipwrights

The word "boat" appears forty-four times in the Gospel accounts. How could Jesus have done the work he did in Israel without boats? He traveled in them, taught from them, and even slept in one. He told his expert-fishermen disciples to let down their net from the other side of their boat. Behind the scenes: boat-builders. Jesus could not have done much of what he did apart from their work.

In 1986, a couple of brothers from a kibbutz in Israel found a first-century boat buried in the mud near Magdala. Thanks to that discovery, we have some insight into boat-building in Jesus' day. According to Jonathan Reed and John Dominic Crossan,

> The hull's strakes and planks were joined with mortise-and-tenon joints, locked together with carefully measured oak pegs, around which pine resin somewhat sealed the wood; a frame hammered in with iron nails and staples stabilized the hull; and the whole underside was smeared with bitumen pitch.[6]

6. Reed and Crossen, "First-Century Galilee Boat."

Professor J. Richard Steffy, of the Institute of Nautical Archaeology at Texas A&M University, studied the ancient boat. He said the methods used to build it resembled what the Mediterranean boatbuilders practiced around that period. Those who built the boat found in the mud near Magdala may have served as apprentices to a Mediterranean shipbuilder.

Stone Carvers

Even in his burial, people blessed Jesus through their work. Taken together, Matthew, Mark, Luke, and John use the word "tomb" thirty-eight times. Scripture tells us that it was Joseph of Arimathea who took Jesus' crucified body and "placed it in his own new tomb that he had cut out of the rock" (Matt 27:60). Chipping a burial vault out of solid stone must have taken an enormous amount of time. The hammering and chiseling had to continue until a large enough cavity had been carved in the rock. It took skill, sweat, and skinned knuckles to create Joseph's gift of a tomb.

So from Jesus' birth to his death, many "invisible" Bible characters blessed him through their work. The list of such people could go on and on. We could add bakers, vintners, farmers, and many more. The point is that Jesus relied on and was blessed by those who did ordinary, everyday work.

Elizabeth Elliot wrote:

> Work is a blessing. God has so arranged the world that work is necessary, and he gives us hands and strength to do it. The enjoyment of leisure would be nothing if we had only leisure. It is the joy of work well done that enables us to enjoy rest, just as it is the experiences of hunger and thirst that make food and drink such pleasures.[7]

Work an evil? A curse? Hardly. Work blesses those who do it. And they in turn bless others through their work.

7. Elliot, *Discipline: The Glad Surrender*, 130.

Discussion

1. Why do you think some people still think of work as evil, coming from God's curse?
2. How has God blessed you through the work you do?
3. How have you been blessed by the work other people do?

For more: Chapter 9 of Nowlen, Jonathan. *Managing Your Metron: A Practical Theology of Work, Mission, and Meaning.* Self-published, 2019.

10

Encouraging Believers

THE PROBLEM SURFACED IN the world's very first workplace. God, the Employer, had tasked Adam with working the soil and taking on the gardener role. That weedless garden-workplace in Eden included an orchard filled with mouth-watering fruit. How could anyone have asked for a better boss or a more pleasant place to work? An ideal situation. God himself had pronounced it all to be good and very good. And yet . . .

In the Genesis account of that seemingly flawless setting, we read that God himself finds something "not good." Just two sentences after giving Adam his job description, God names the missing element in that workplace: it was "not good" for Adam to be alone. The three-in-one God had never been alone—always enjoying a mutually supportive love relationship. So it would not do for the man made in his image to go it solo.

Since the day sin invaded the planet in Genesis 3, no workplace in the world has even begun to measure up to that first one. This side of Eden, impossible deadlines, treacherous coworkers, narcissistic bosses, computer viruses, obsolete equipment, and much more confront today's labor force. On top of these pressures, Christians may undergo incoming hostility to any expression of biblical faith. In such a workplace furnace, it is not good to face the heat alone.

The Lonely Christian at Work

A. W. Tozer wrote:

> The loneliness of the Christian results from his walk with God in an ungodly world, a walk that must often take him away from the fellowship of good Christians . . . His God-given instincts cry out for companionship with others of his kind, others who can understand his longings, his aspirations, his absorption in the love of Christ; and because within his circle of friends there are so few who share his inner experiences he is forced to walk alone.[1]

Centuries ago, Elijah twice told God, "I am the only one left" (1 Kgs 19:10, 14). Today, Christ followers—surrounded by coworkers who do not share and may even spurn the faith—can work under that same "only one left" cloud.

Such Christians live and work in what we might call "spiritual exile." This isolation offers yet another motive for those who follow Jesus to get up and go to work: *to encourage and build up fellow believers.* To let them know that, no, they are not alone in the struggle.

Our Call to Encourage Each Other

The New Testament brims with examples of encouragement. And it calls us to serve as encouragers within the family of God. For instance: "Encourage one another" (1 Thess 5:11). "Encourage the disheartened" (1 Thess 5:14). "Encourage one another daily" (Heb 3:13). In this last example, the author of Hebrews explains the need for such constant and repeated support: "so that none of you may be hardened by sin's deceitfulness."

1. Tozer, *Man, the Dwelling Place of God*, 192.

Sin's deceitfulness saturates the work world. Working in that environment day-in-day-out, week-in-week-out, threatens to petrify the tender hearts of even the most sincere Christians. But fellow members of Christ's body can serve as softening agents—Christians who, filled with his own Spirit, come alongside others with words and acts of encouragement, backing, and care.

But even among Christ followers, that kind of encouragement does not take place nearly often enough in the world of work. Why not?

From Church-Centric to Kingdom-Centric

For decades, I held a severely anemic interpretation of "encourage one another daily" (Heb 3:13). I knew that "one another" meant fellow Christ followers. But, in effect, I built a silo around those two words. That is, I pretty much confined "one another" to mean those in the church group I met with on weekends.

Honestly, of course, it was difficult if not impossible to encourage daily those in my church crowd. For at least three reasons. One, there were far too many of them to contact that often. Two, the bulk of those in the Sunday crowd remained strangers to me—I had never met most of them. And three, even for the few I knew, Sunday was the only day our paths crossed. Many lived and worked ten, thirty, or fifty miles away.

Thankfully, my interpretation of Hebrews 3:13 expanded when I finally stopped reading it through the narrow lens of the institutional, gathered church. Instead, I began seeing it through the wide-angle lens of the kingdom of God. In the close-up view, those to be encouraged all came from pretty much the same denominational "tribe." But in the panoramic, kingdom-of-God view, Christ followers belonged to all kinds of clans—many in denominations, many others with no denominational ties.

And into that wider, more inclusive viewfinder came coworkers and neighbors next door and down the street. These were the Christians I was likely to know and see on more than just Sundays.

From what I can observe, most of us do not think of encouraging fellow believers as one of the main reasons to get up and go to work.

Encouragement Possible in Today's Work World

Given the state of our world today, with its political correctness and faith-aversion, is such expansive encouragement even possible on the job? Yes, according to Jason, a Facebook employee stationed in Seattle.

As of December 2020, Facebook employed nearly fifty-nine thousand employees in eighty-two locations around the world. Jason estimates that at least two thousand of these are Christ followers. Facebook, along with other social media giants such as Google, Instagram, and Twitter, has been accused of bias and censorship. So can Christians working for Facebook find a place and a voice?

In the Seattle area, one to two hundred Christ followers work in multiple buildings. In their various conference rooms, believers begin their week in a Monday-morning prayer meeting, interceding for each other, for coworkers, and the company itself. On Thursdays, those in the Puget Sound area rotate in leading a book study each Thursday. Recent topics: practicing faith at work, the relationship of faith to technology, and how cell phones are changing our minds, activities, and habits. Across the US West Coast, Facebook believers meet online for a Bible study every Friday noon over lunch.

I asked Jason if they had encountered any resistance from Facebook. To the contrary: "Facebook supports and encourages faith-based groups to meet," he said.

Jason is enthusiastic about the benefits of Christians meeting in their workplace groups. "For me personally," he said, "it really helps to know that I am not alone. There are two or three Christians right on my team. The Monday-morning prayer meeting sets the tone for the rest of the week."

In their various meetings, Christians are able to share articles on theology, discuss struggles and how they are handling them, and personal testimonies of what they have been through. Visiting speakers have helped them overcome the sacred-secular divide. When someone is undergoing a particularly difficult time, others come alongside and pray for them.

The Facebook Christian group is just one among many. The Faith & Work Movement, which began in Silicon Valley, now extends around the world. From its website:

> We have interacted with more than 100 companies and developed workplace fellowship leaders networks in San Francisco, Austin, Chicago, Seattle, London, Dublin, and Singapore. We are a growing global alliance of people called to the workplace . . .
>
> We exist to positively impact companies that impact the world and to help Christians in the marketplace to bring their best self to work. We do this by honoring God at work, encouraging one another, loving our coworkers the way Jesus would if he had our jobs, and praying for companies, leaders, each other, and our cities.[2]

One-on-One Encouragement

Encouraging fellow believers on the job need not be confined to formal times of meeting in person or online. A friend of mine worked in a department that raises funds for a large hospital. She mentioned how a Christian janitor had noticed she seemed exhausted. How could he pray for her? he asked. Might he share her need—minus her name—with other believers in the hospital? She agreed.

Hearing this much, I wanted to learn the rest of the story. With her help, I arranged a meeting with the janitor. He told me he had worked in the environmental services department of this hospital for twenty-two years. But he did not originally intend to work in this role. I'll let him tell his own story.

> I was heading toward the ministry, so I completed regular Bible college and seminary training. But while I thought I was going to be a pastor, things did not work out that way. So I returned to what I had done to earn my way

2. Faith and Work Movement, "Our Story."

through school: janitorial work in this hospital. But I was not happy in this role. I tried hard to get into something else—anything else.

Thinking I might become a chaplain, I enrolled in a clinical pastoral education training program in another hospital. During my second quarter there, I visited an older patient who had served as a pastor. As I spoke with him, I must have voiced some negativity about being a janitor and not in the ministry. He looked me straight in the eye and said, "But you are in the ministry." God used his words to change my whole attitude. Suddenly, I no longer looked at the hospital as just a place to work. Since that time, God has used me in many ways in people's lives—ways I could never have imagined.

One man (I'll call him Frank), a fellow janitor, had been an alcoholic. He had divorced his Christian wife. But sometime after that, he had opened his heart to Jesus. In time, he married a wonderful Christian woman who also works here at the hospital. I urged him to memorize Scripture. "No," he said, "I can't memorize. My education ended in grade school." But I persisted, starting him with a few basic verses. He found out he *could* memorize God's word. As he grew, I discovered he had a real gift in dealing with people.

My work puts me into contact with many people, and that's where the momentum of this ministry lies. God has placed me where I can talk to others, learn their needs and ask, "Would you like us to pray?" On any given day, I can usually get to ten or fifteen believers in the prayer chain. All told, I probably know of thirty to forty believers in the various hospital departments.

My seminary training doesn't really enter into this hospital ministry. The Holy Spirit helps me find ways to break the ice. When I worked in the surgery area, I used to ask the surgeons, "What is the most amazing part of the human body?" Most answered with that part of the body they had specialized in. Then I would ask, "How can anybody believe all this just happened?" Almost all responded that they didn't know. But one surgeon said, "I know—God created it!" And of course I had just discovered a fellow believer!

> This ministry has blossomed in ways that have benefited my family. It's not unusual for me to return home and tell my wife and kids, "Okay, we need to pray for this or that person." Had I chosen my own way, I would now be pastoring a church. But this, not that, was what God wanted me to do. Knowing that, I need to do my work well. I'm here to serve—and that's what "ministry" means.

Discovering Fellow Christians at Work

The work of this janitor takes him from office to office, where he buoys up working Christians. His job is unique in that he encounters quite a sizable number of coworkers each day. But whether the number be large or small, the need to encourage fellow Christ followers holds true in almost all kinds of work roles.

A few years ago, I surveyed sixty Christians in non-church-related jobs. Those responding came from rural, suburban, and inner city churches. One of the survey questions asked: "How many other believers are you aware of among those you interact with at work (coworkers, clients, customers, students, etc.)?" Nearly half said they knew of six or more Christians in their work networks. Only three (just five percent) were unaware of any Christians on the job.

The next question in my survey asked, "If you do know of other believers where you work, do you deliberately seek opportunities to encourage them in their faith and walk?" Here, the responses were virtually even, with half saying yes and half no. For those saying yes, serving other members of the Body of Christ provided a strong reason to get up and go to work.

I did not follow up with the half who said no. Why did they not intentionally reach out to encourage Christian coworkers? It is possible that some of them may have been at a loss as to how to discover fellow believers among those they worked with. In a typical church setting, we do not develop "Christian-detector" skills. We simply take it for granted those who attend regularly are Christ followers.

To seek out other Christians in the workplace, the obvious place to begin is prayer, asking the Lord to direct our encounters and to help us discern those seeking to follow him.

Christeen Rico, an Apple employee, suggests two ways to find fellow believers on the job. First, she suggests sending a message out to the company Slack channels or other internal employee communication platforms. The message could ask: "Are there any Christians here who'd be willing to get together for lunch?" Second, she recommends asking pastors or church leaders if they know anyone who works in the same company.

A deliberate effort to find fellow believers among coworkers might mean preparing a few questions to ask during normal conversations. For example:

- How would you describe your priorities?
- What books might you be reading?
- Who is your most-admired hero?

If the responses to such questions seem promising, they may open the way to further revealing dialogue. The goal is to find even one or two others serious about living out their faith on the job. They may well know other Christians working in the same company or vicinity. In this way, the group for mutual encouragement can multiply.

But typically, most of those around us at work are not trusting or following Jesus. So our call includes serving non-Christians as well. As Paul urged the Galatians, "As we have opportunity, let us do good to all people, especially to those who belong to the family of believers" (Gal 6:10).

Discussion

1. How have other Christians in your workplace encouraged you or spurred you on?
2. How many other Christians are you aware of in your working contacts (coworkers, bosses, vendors, students, patients, etc.)?
3. In what ways could you and the Christians you know through your work expand the circle?

For more: Chapter 7 of Peabody, Larry. *Job-Shadowing Daniel: Walking the Talk at Work*. Denver: Outskirts, 2010.

11

Embodying Truth

It happened one day while I was working as an information assistant for the state highways department in our state. A man I'll call Marc was part of a Bible study group that met in my office during the lunch hour. Since our group was no secret, others in the agency had come to identify him with our gathering.

The internal walls of our office building were made of painted steel. As it happened, I was rounding the corner from a main hallway into one that crossed it. That's when I saw Marc. He had pinned a non-Christian in the right angle formed by the steel wall and one side of a Coke machine. Marc was "witnessing" away at the cornered man with some clearly unwelcomed intensity. Suddenly, my face felt flushed. I was embarrassed to be identified with this fellow Christian.

Why would Marc have resorted to such coercive tactics? I suspect at least two ideas were driving him, ideas that trouble others as well. One, he felt compelled to speak the gospel on the job. And two, in his mind "witnessing" had been reduced to one thing—vocalizing the gospel to unbelievers. He may have bought into the idea that voicing the good news is God's only reason for keeping us on earth.

A Catch-22

Here's the rub: If our sole purpose on earth is witnessing, and if witnessing only means speaking the gospel to unbelievers, then those in the workplace are in trouble.

Why? Because employers pay us to do our jobs, not to talk about Jesus. If we think God has us there only to present the gospel, we end up in a double bind. On the one hand, if we steal paid hours to evangelize, we will lose respect and credibility with bosses and coworkers. On the other hand, if we don't evangelize on the job, we will work under a cloud of guilt.

How can we escape this Catch-22? Is there a word that will fit the workplace context and still convey the responsibility of all Christ followers to serve as his witnesses? I believe the term "embody" accomplishes both. The "em-" part of that word means "to put into." That "em-" prefix gives us words like:

- *Empathize*—to put oneself into what others feel.
- *Emplace*—to put into position.
- *Empower*—to put into a place of authority.

Embody, then, means to put into a body.

We Christians have a big theological word for embodiment: "incarnation"—a putting into flesh. Christ said to his Father, "a body you prepared for me" (Heb 10:5). Many New Testament passages refer to Christ's coming "in the flesh," meaning in a body.

The Embodied Christ

In bringing the gospel to us on earth, God did not set up loudspeakers in orbiting satellites to blare the message from space. Instead, he sent his Son inside a human body. Jesus was *embodied.* Put into a body. He was not just a speaking mouth. His body had arms and legs and shoulders and elbows and ears and smiles and frowns. So those around him not only heard what he said but could also watch his actions and reactions, reading his body language.

Think of the actions Jesus took that he could not have done without a human body.

- Hands: He washed and dried the feet of his disciples (John 13:5).
- Feet: He allowed a sinful woman to wash his feet with her tears (Luke 7:38).
- Eyes: He shed tears at Lazarus's grave (John 11:35).
- Ears: When he asked questions, he listened to the answers (Luke 22:35, 36).
- Mouth: He ate with sinners (Mark 2:13–17).

When Jesus welcomed guests into his home, they observed his hospitality (John 1:35–39). His disciples saw him refuse to take revenge (Luke 9:51–56). They noted how he acted when in danger (Mark 4:35–39). People saw how he behaved when he was tired and hungry. They watched him boarding boats, walking on footpaths, climbing a mountain, and riding a donkey.

No wonder, then, that when John, his closest disciple, was describing their experience with Jesus, he wrote about that "which we have heard, which we have seen with our eyes, which we have looked at and our hands have touched—this we proclaim concerning the Word of life" (1 John 1:1). In other words, they knew Jesus *embodied.*

Body Work

Today, we who know, love, and trust Jesus are the dwelling places of Christ's Spirit. So we *embody* him. Our witness will engage not only our mouths, but our eyes, ears, hands, and feet—all the members of our bodies. Having a job typically puts us side by side with unbelievers. Day after day, week after week, month after month, right before their eyes, they should see the evidence of the inner Christ-life lived out through our bodies.

Embodying Christ, the Truth, fits the workplace—because the work we do gets done by means of our bodies. If you pilot a ferry, you engage your eyes, ears, hands, feet, voice, and so on. If you work as a traffic flagger, you use your brain, eyes, hands, and more. Whether you do manual or mental work, you do it as an embodied person.

When Jesus tells us how to let his light shine out into the surrounding spiritual darkness, we might think he would emphasize witnessing with our words. But no, he does something unexpected. Listen as he explains the way: "Let your light shine before others, that they may see your good deeds and glorify your Father in heaven" (Matt 5:16). In the Greek original, those good deeds are "good works." Work! Exactly what we are called to do on the job.

Notice how Andrew Murray describes two distinctly different roles within the body of Christ:

> It is in the power of the omnipotent Savior that the believer must find strength for life and for work . . . With **some** the chief testimony was to be that of a holy life revealing heaven and Christ as its source. The power came to set up the Kingdom within them, to give victory over sin and self, to fit them by living experience to testify to the power of Jesus on the throne and to make men live in the world as saints. **Others** were to give themselves up entirely to speaking in the name of Jesus. But **all** needed and **all** received the same gift of power in order to prove that Jesus had now received the Kingdom of the father and all power in heaven and earth was indeed given to him. And this power was imparted to his people just as they needed it, whether for a holy life or effective service.[1]

The work of some will mainly involve *voicing* the good news about Jesus. The income of these Christians often comes from the giving of believers in the work world. The work of others will mainly call for *showing* the truth as it is in Jesus through what they do and how they do it. Naturally, those voicing the gospel are to show it, and those showing the truth are to voice it as opportunities come.

1. Murray, *Abide in Christ*, 97. Emphasis added.

Those opportunities may come as questions. Why do you live and work the way you do? How could you forgive so-and-so for what they did to you? We need to prayerfully consider how to respond. David Gill understands this: "At some point after lots of listening and caring and (we hope and pray) understanding, we may get a chance to speak. Understanding, empathy, compassion, and comfort are the first and most important things to communicate."[2]

Translucent Work

We should not expect to see any completely external difference in most lines of work between how conscientious Christians and non-Christians get the work itself done. If the work is accounting, the Christ-follower and the atheist will carry on that activity by following the same generally accepted accounting principles. A Christian and a Muslim forklift driver will both run their machines with steering wheels, pedals, and levers.

How, then, can our work be translucent—letting the light shine through it? In the attitudes, relationships, and responses with which it is done. Notice how Paul instructs first-century slaves to demonstrate Spirit-led work in Ephesians 6:5–8 and Colossians 3:22–25. We are called to show respect for those over us—and not just while they are present. No apple-polishing with the boss. God expects us to comply with instructions. We are to engage wholeheartedly with our tasks. And we work in hope, knowing that the Lord will reward our good work.

In *The "Jesus Family" in Communist China*, D. Vaughan Rees wrote that Chinese believers "looked upon labor as a sacred trust, which was to be done for God." While in China, he was given a personal attendant to look after his needs. Rees said this Chinese man "did the most menial jobs for me, jobs which I never asked of him. When I thanked him he told me straight out that being thanked

2. Gill, *Workplace Discipleship 101*, 170.

rather dulled the keen edge of his service for the Lord . . . He told me that *his work was his only method of preaching*."[3]

To put it a bit differently, this Chinese man, by embodying the Truth in his work, made the way of God known.

God Can Even Use Jokes

The thirty-acre farm was not supporting our family of six. In one whole year, Dad had realized only $450 from the sale of crops. So he did what he had to do—he took a job in a town about six miles away. The company owned by his employer manufactured farm equipment. Because Dad was a skilled welder and had designed and built machinery for his own farm, the job was a good fit.

But he soon discovered that he did not fit in with the way the men talked on breaks and lunch hours. The agenda almost always involved a competition to see who could tell the most knee-slapping, off-color joke. At first, as a committed Christ follower, Dad withdrew and spent those off-duty periods by himself. But the Spirit of God began letting him know that isolation was not the way to go.

So he made it a project to find and memorize some hilarious but clean stories. Joke-telling did not come naturally to Dad, but he persisted. Then, rejoining the men during break times, he would weave his untarnished yarns into the conversation. In time, he noticed that the other guys in the shop were bringing more wholesome tales and even cleaned up their language. This change came about because of the presence of a human body inhabited by the Spirit of God.

Embodied truth.

3. Rees, *"Jesus Family" in Communist China*, in Peabody, *Serving Christ in the Workplace*, 66.

Discussion

1. Have you sensed that God's main reason for having you in the workplace is to speak the gospel to unbelievers at work? Why do you think you felt that way?
2. If someone asked you what "embodying truth" means, what would you say?
3. In the workplace context, is the idea of "embodying truth" for unbelievers more helpful or less helpful than that of "witnessing to" them? Why?

For more: Chapter 5 of Bernbaum, John A., and Simon M. Steer. *Why Work: Careers and Employment in Biblical Perspective.* Grand Rapids, MI: Baker, 1986.

12

Call to Action

LET'S SAY YOU'RE AN accountant. A large retail chain reaches out for someone with your exact qualifications. You respond, and they call you to begin work on Monday. When you arrive, the company provides you with an office and a set of tools—*a table saw, a belt sander, and a drill press.* "No way!" you say. Any company wanting to stay in business would issue tools that fit the job it calls people to do.

In the same way, when God—who is infinitely wiser than any corporation—calls us, he equips us with gifts suitable to his calling.

What Is a Calling?

In the 2007 film *Freedom Writers*, Erin Gruwell (played by Hilary Swank) is a teacher working with at-risk students in Long Beach, California. After working long hours through many precarious moments, she finally sees her class responding. Gruwell explains her motivation to her husband: "I finally realized what I'm supposed to be doing, and I love it. When I'm helping those kids make sense of their lives, everything about my life makes sense to me."[1]

1. LaGravenese, *Freedom Writers*.

Without using the word, Gruwell was saying she had discovered her calling. Do only Christians have callings? No, non-Christians can come to know theirs too, even if they do not know the Caller. The image of God in them means they were made for a purpose.

The Calling-Gift Matchup

Even before I enrolled in Wheaton College, several Christians had already told me God had given me a teaching gift. Then, in my sophomore year in college, I completed a creative writing class, where I discovered both an affinity and aptitude for writing.

Fast forward to three years after graduation from college. I responded to an ad to work as an information officer for the Washington State Department of Highways. This job mostly involved writing. While I served in this role, a verse from Isaiah enlarged my understanding of God's purpose for my life. My calling would include the work of restoring God-given truths the centuries have buried.

In time, I was asked to plant and shepherd a church—a role involving both teaching and writing. And now, for the past several years, I have instructed grad-school students in the theology of work. So, I'm still teaching and writing, still using gifts that fit my calling. Jobs and roles changed. Yet my calling—reminding God's people of truth lost to sight—remained constant. And my God-given gifts matched my calling.

What about you? How can you begin to discover God's intent for your life?

1. God's Calling Need Not Be Dramatic

Steer clear of the notion that God's calling must be spectacular. Yes, his calling of Paul and Isaiah came suddenly and dramatically. But in the lives of Joseph and Daniel, God used painful events in revealing their callings.

Well into his career, Joseph could honestly tell his brothers, "It was to save lives that God sent me ahead of you" (Gen 45:5). How did Joseph experience God's calling to serve him as a government official in Egypt?

His brothers, who hated him, nearly killed him and then threw him into a cistern. When a band of traders happened along, his brothers sold him to them. He landed in Egypt as the slave of Potiphar, who put him in charge of his household. After Potiphar's wife falsely accused him of rape, Joseph went to prison. There, while working as a trusted inmate, he favorably and correctly interpreted the dream of the pharaoh's chief cupbearer. Although Joseph asked him to tell the pharaoh that he had been falsely imprisoned, the cupbearer forgot him.

After two full years, when the pharaoh himself needed someone to interpret a dream, the cupbearer's memory improved. He recommended Joseph, who interpreted the pharaoh's dream. This led to his being named as prime minister of Egypt. So how did God call come to Joseph? Through circumstances—extremely painful ones.

Or recall Daniel's situation. He might have known Jeremiah. If so, it's possible he had heard others or Jeremiah himself describe his call. You might say Jeremiah's calling was dramatic. God had said to him, "Before I formed you in the womb I knew you, before you were born I set you apart; I appointed you as a prophet to the nations" (Jer 1:5). Now that's exciting—to know that God had that kind of reason for creating you. A word from God like that gives purpose for one's life.

But what about Daniel's calling? From all outward signs, it looks as if his came from the gritty fact of war. His being captured and hauled off as a prisoner to Babylon makes it seem like Daniel was not placed but *dis*placed. What if Daniel had told himself, "God spoke directly to Jeremiah. His call came from God's voice. I heard no voice. Jeremiah's call made him a prophet; my circumstances made me into a bureaucrat. I guess God hasn't called me into ministry"? And yet Daniel wrote a vitally important book in the Bible, and Jesus called him a prophet (Matt 24:15).

For most people, the perception of God's calling comes through a growing understanding of who and where they are—a bit like discovering the pattern in a woven rug. The seemingly ordinary threads—including circumstantial ones—seen together begin to form a picture.

2. *God's Calling Is for All Christians*

Don't buy the idea that God calls people only into church-related work. In *The Other Six Days*, R. Paul Stevens says, "Almost the only people who speak of being 'called of God' are 'full-time' pastors and missionaries."[2] Since the word *calling* has become so closely linked to clergy, it may help to think of calling in terms of God's *purpose* for your life. What does God intend for you to accomplish here on his earth? Paul says those who love God "have been called"—there's the calling word—"according to his purpose" (Rom 8:28).

So calling does not have to come with fireworks. Nor does it have to launch us into what many see as "spiritual" work.

3. *Gifts Help Reveal God's Calling*

A set of keys may prove useful as you unlock insights into your calling/purpose. As suggested in the opening illustration, if a company calls an accountant to work for it, you'd expect the firm to provide the right tools—such as a computer and a spreadsheet program. In a similar way, by sorting through the "tools" God has given us, we can begin to collect clues that will help us see what he has designed us to do.

Ask yourself questions like these. What motivates me? What makes me lose track of time while I'm doing it? What am I good at doing—in other words, what is my gift set? What describes my personality? Do I prefer to work alone or as part of a team? Asking questions like these will help you discover what God has put into your toolbox.

2. Stevens, *Other Six Days*, 72.

Is that biblical? Does God's calling really go hand-in-glove with his gifting? Consider Bezalel. He rubbed shoulders with Moses, but their two callings differed dramatically. God called Moses to lead the Israelites out of slavery in Egypt and through the wilderness on their way to the promised land. To equip him for that calling, God gave Moses miraculous gifts—think of the ten plagues, water from a rock, manna from heaven, and so on.

By contrast, God called Bezalel to design and build the tabernacle and all its furniture. So what kind of gifts did God give him? Here's how God himself put it: "I have filled him with the Spirit of God, with skill, ability and knowledge in all kinds of crafts—to make artistic designs for work in gold, silver and bronze, to cut and set stones, to work in wood, and to engage in all kinds of craftsmanship" (Ex 31:3–5).

What was God's purpose for him? Through Bezalel God wanted to provide a tabernacle in the wilderness for his people. Bezalel's gifts, given by God's Spirit, tallied with God's call or purpose for him. In terms of God's purpose, Bezalel's gifts and calling were just as vital as those of Moses.

In her final paper, a student in my theology-of-work course described part of her own gift-discovery process:

> I was sitting in church eighteen years ago, and I heard a question in my head. It seemingly came out of nowhere and had nothing to do with the sermon I was listening to. The question was, "What is something you do that you never consciously think about. It is simply so ingrained in you that it emerges consistently?" The answer came to me quickly. I connect. I connect people to people and I connect with others. Even when I am not trying to do so. It began in second grade, with kids seeking me out to tell me something they had "never told anyone else." And it continued through college and into my professional life. I suspect God was calling me to live out "connection" in a deliberate way for him.

Let's recap. One, God's call need not come in some sudden or breathtaking way. Two, God calls all Christians, not just pastors and missionaries. Three, God equips—he gives tools that fit his calling.

4. God's Calling and Gifts for the Scattered Church

Finally, God's purposes include what happens in both the gathered and the scattered church. Those who have been around churches for any length of time know that spiritual-gift inventories usually focus on gifts for use inside the gathered church. Every Christian has received at least one gift for that purpose.

But many remain unaware that God also gives gifts for serving him in the *scattered* church. After a Sunday church meeting ends, its people spread out on Monday into all kinds of places throughout a community. Into hospitals, government agencies, schools, homes, shops, offices, farms, factories, and so on. Because God is sovereign over and cares about his whole creation—not just the gathered-church part of it—he gives gifts that make people able to serve outside the gathering.

Daniel and his three Jewish friends were taken from their homeland to serve in the government of Babylon. Listen to how the Bible says God gifted them:

> To these four young men God gave [gifted them with] knowledge and understanding of all kinds of literature and learning . . . The king [Nebuchadnezzar] talked with them, and he found none equal to Daniel, Hananiah, Mishael and Azariah; so they entered the king's service. In every matter of wisdom and understanding about which the king questioned them, he found them ten times better than all the magicians and enchanters in his whole kingdom. (Dan 1:17, 19–20)

God-given gifts for work in a secular government!

In the book of Jeremiah, God calls Nebuchadnezzar, the king of pagan Babylon, "my servant" no less than three times. So Daniel and his friends—while working for the government there—were actually serving the servant of God. They were helping

Nebuchadnezzar care for that piece of God's real estate we now call Iraq.

What have we seen? First, God's call may not come in any miraculous way. Second, God's calling is for all his people—not just those in "full-time Christian service." Third, a Christian's motivations, abilities, and personality can serve as clues for discovering God's calling. And fourth, God gives gifts not only for use in the gathered but also in the scattered church.

Partners Help in Calling/Gift Discovery

On your own, you can begin that process of reflecting on how God has made you. But let's admit it: everyone has blind spots. So why not enlist two or three Christian friends to help you take inventory? These should be people who have known you well enough to respond from longstanding observation.

Ask them: *What do you see as my gifts? What do you think motivates me? What are my strengths and weaknesses?* Then encourage them to ask God to help them process what they hear as they seek to understand his calling on your life.

The Pulling-Power of Calling

US President Dwight Eisenhower once said, "Pull the string and it will follow you wherever you go. Push it and it will go nowhere at all."[3] That's the power of knowing God's call or purpose for our lives. Like a magnet pulling iron, God's purpose tugs us forward. The more we respond to the drawing power of God's purpose, the less we will be pushed this way and that by our own wrong desires, our insecurities, or what others may think of us.

We are not to be pushovers. God's call pulls us forward, so that in the end it can be said of each of us, as Scripture says about David: "When David had served God's purpose in his own

3. Kinkade, "Futility of Pushing a String . . ."

generation, he fell asleep" (Acts 13:36). What is God's purpose for you? Are you being pushed or pulled?

Discussion

1. How would you explain why so many Christians remain unsure of their callings?
2. If you believe you understand God's calling for your life, describe how he revealed it to you.
3. In what way do your God-given gifts mesh with your calling?

For more: Chapter 4 of Stevens, R. Paul. *The Other Six Days*. Grand Rapids, MI: Eerdmans, 2016.

13

Working to Obey

The idea seemed perfectly clear to me when I enrolled in Wheaton College. Obeying God in my work would mean serving him as a pastor or missionary. No one had actually taught me to think that way in so many words. Instead, I caught the idea—a bit like catching a cold or the flu.

Maybe I had been exposed to the virus by noticing how other church people raved about the work of my missionary uncle. Yet when it came to the work of my farmer father . . . silence. Or maybe it happened during a farewell event for our pastor when I was twelve. His wife pulled me aside and said, "Larry, we're expecting to hear great things from you." Those were her words. But I knew what she meant: "Larry, we're expecting you to go into full-time Christian service when you grow up."

The idea took root in me. I arrived in Wheaton convinced that I should either pastor a church in my own country or cross an ocean as a missionary. But in my sophomore year, something strange and troubling began to take place deep inside me. I sensed a gentle urging to enter the everyday work world where most Christ followers live out the prime-time hours of their lives.

The mismatch between that inner urging and my mind-set about doing church work became more and more intense. Finally, I sat down and wrote out a two-page argument with God. The dialogue took on the format of a playscript:

Larry: ". . ."
God: ". . ."
Larry: ". . ."
God: ". . ."

By page two, I began to sense I was losing the argument. The last two lines of dialogue went like this:

Larry: "But what will happen to me if I do go into secular work? Will I just disappear and become a nobody in some commuter shuffle?"

God: "If you can wait, you will see."

A few years later, when I began working as an information officer for a state government agency, I did so as an act of obedience to what God was calling me to do.

God-Given Commands to Work

To obey is to act on a call to do something. Work as obedience carries out what God calls for. When Moses led the Israelites out of Egypt and they camped out at Mt. Sinai, God spoke about work. In the fourth of the Ten Commandments, he said, "Six days you shall labor and do all your work" (Exod 20:9). Think of it! It was God who came up with the seven-day week. And here he tells his people to spend almost 86 percent of those days . . . *working*!

This command to work gets repeated:

- "Six days do your work" (Exod 23:12).
- "Six days you shall labor and do all your work" (Deut 5:13).

And in the New Testament, God's work command lies behind much of what Paul wrote in his letters to churches: You should "mind your own business and work with your hands" (1 Thess

4:11). Paul himself obeyed what he preached. His calloused hands got dirty in the tent-manufacturing business.

Paul had heard reports of unproductive Christians in Thessalonica. In his words, they were "idle and disruptive" (1 Thess 5:14; 2 Thess 3:11–12). They were "not busy." So he instructed them to "settle down and earn" their food. He even went so far as to say any Christian unwilling to obey God by working should be barred from eating.

Right from the beginning and throughout the Bible, working is a fundamental way we obey God. That alone should be enough to get us out of bed and send us out to our work. But while this obedience reason would be enough on its own, there are many more reasons for working, as other chapters emphasize.

What Is Your Calendar Telling You?

Do you see your work as obeying God? You switch on your computer and open your weekly calendar. Monday has no entries. You'll just be at work that day. No entries either for Tuesday morning or afternoon (work again), but for Tuesday evening, you have entered the time you plan to spend with your weekly Bible-study group.

Same story during daytime hours on Wednesday (at work). But that evening shows a church dinner—an event featuring a missionary speaker just returned from Kenya. Blank spaces signal work again Thursday. But, as the calendar reminds you, after work you've committed yourself to drive the church van, shuttling the youth group to a concert. Friday at 6 p.m., you and your family are planning on dinner out.

At which of those times during this week will you be motivated by conscious obedience to God?

- While doing church-related activities?
- At dinner with your family?
- On the job?
- All three?

A Work Parable

As he did so often, Jesus told a story that involved working. He told this one to the Jewish religious leaders. The story went like this: A farmer father asked his two sons to get up and go to work in his grape field.

The first son flatly said no. But after thinking it over, he changed his mind and went to work. The second son, hearing the same assignment from Dad, agreed right away to do so. But in the end, he never showed up at the work site.

Jesus then asked this question: "Which of the two did what the father wanted?" (Matt 21:31). The answer is obvious. When the father said, "Go to work," the first son obeyed—even if not right away. He demonstrated his obedience by going to work.

While Jesus applied this parable one way, I think we can safely apply it in another. Our Father in heaven has made his will clear: he tells us to work in his field, his world. So if we love and want to please him, we will do as he says. Our primary reason for getting up and going to work—paid or unpaid—will be to obey him.

Some Love Their Work

You've probably heard advice, from those widely regarded as experts, urging us to love our work:

- Various people are reported to have said: "Choose a job you love, and you will never have to work a day in your life."
- The co-founder of Apple, Steve Jobs, said, "The only way to do great work is to love what you do. If you haven't found it yet, keep looking. Don't settle."[1]

I can appreciate the sentiment behind those love-your-work statements. Even Dorothy Sayers, in her essay "Why Work?" urges workers to think of their work "as a creative activity undertaken for the love of the work itself."

1. Goodreads, "Steve Jobs."

Others Don't Care for Their Work

It seems, though, that while many people love the work they do, far more find themselves in jobs they will never love—and sometimes hate. Gallup, the polling company, has tracked down various levels of employee engagement. Drawing from the results of their research, they place employees in one of these three categories:

- *Engaged* employees immerse themselves in and are excited about their work.
- Those *not engaged* don't put their hearts into their jobs and probably do just enough to get by.
- The *actively disengaged* have a negative connection with where they work and what they do—an attitude that infects their work and that of others around them.

The levels of engagement fluctuate slightly from year to year. But a 2021 Gallup poll found 35–36 percent of US workers to be "engaged" in their workplaces. This left nearly two-thirds either not engaged or actively disengaged from their work.[2] Many, even though they do not love it, stay with their work for other reasons. Maybe they need the regular paycheck. Or perhaps they can't find any other work.

Can everyone love their work? No. But all of us are commanded, as Jesus reminds us, to "Love the Lord your God with all your heart and with all your soul and with all your mind and with all your strength" (Mark 12:30). Real love for God results in obeying him. "If you love me," Jesus says, "keep my commands" (John 14:15).

Jesus: Our Example of Obedient Work

Jesus practiced what he preached. When it comes to obeying God in our work, we can find no better example than Jesus himself. No less than thirty-eight times, Jesus says "sent me," referring to

2. Harter, "US Employee Engagement Rises Following Wild 2020."

his own work assignment from his Father (Matt 10:40). When his disciples found him talking to a Samaritan woman at the well, they offered him food. When Jesus refused, he explained his mission in the world: "My food . . . is to do the will of him who sent me and to finish his work" (John 4:34).

Like the son who went to work in his father's grape field, Jesus obeyed—coming to his Father's world/field/workplace as a human being. Paul said it better than anyone else when he wrote of Jesus:

> Who, being in very nature God,
> did not consider equality with God
> something to be used to his own advantage;
> rather, he made himself nothing
> by taking the very nature of a servant,
> being made in human likeness.
> And being found in appearance as a man,
> he humbled himself
> by becoming obedient to death—
> even death on a cross!
> Therefore God exalted him to the highest place
> and gave him the name that is above every name,
> that at the name of Jesus every knee should bow,
> in heaven and on earth and under the earth,
> and every tongue acknowledge that Jesus Christ is Lord,
> to the glory of God the Father. (Phil 2:6–11)

Jesus came as a servant—one who works for someone else. He offered no half-hearted obedience. Obeying his Father took him all the way to that painful death on that humiliating cross. And just before going to that cross, he told his Father, "I have brought you glory on earth by finishing the work you gave me to do" (John 17:4).

Jesus not only saves us; he also models for us what we should be and do. How should we teach? Watch Jesus as he tells stories and asking questions. How should we relate to each other? Watch as Jesus serves his disciples by washing their feet. How should we pray for those who wrong us? Watch Jesus who, after being beaten and nailed to his cross, prays, "Father, forgive them" (Luke 23:34).

Watching Jesus at work provides us with patterns for doing our work.

Why Get Up and Go to Work? To Obey God

Some may question whether obedience to God should top the list of our reasons for working. The objection might be expressed like this: "At work, I do exactly the same things my atheist and agnostic coworkers do. Obeying God is the last thing that motivates them . . . And they are certainly not working to obey God."

Granted. But what if they are obeying God without even knowing it?

As we've seen in chapter 2, when God created human beings, he gave one reason for doing so: that we should take charge of his earthly real estate and its creatures. But how? Through what activity would we carry out that taking charge?

Through work. How do we know that? After planting the Garden of Eden, God assigned Adam to "work it and take care of it" (Gen 2:15). Some call this assignment God's "first commission" for the human race. All legitimate work, in some way, contributes to making earth a livable place to be. But through our working we carry out God's will in other ways.

"But My Work Seems So Ordinary . . ."

How, you might be asking, does my going to work matter to God? I balance budgets. Or I wire houses. Or I sell insurance. How is my kind of working an obedience that helps to carry out God's will on earth?

Most work, whether paid or unpaid, gets us out and about. It puts us in touch with other people. When the work of a stay-at-home mom takes her to the grocery store, she interacts with the employees and with other customers. When the work of a plumber takes him into a home with leaky pipes, he relates to the homeowners.

The point? Through their work, God scatters his Christ-following people far and wide. Jesus said we are "good seed." We are the "people of the kingdom" (Matt 13:38). Through the prophet Zechariah, God says, "Though I have scattered them like seeds among the nations, they will still remember me in distant lands" (Zech 10:9, NLT). We seeds have been sown in the land all over the place—infiltrating communities around the globe. So God intends that each Christian, in his or her work, take up that post as an agent of God's kingdom.

Jesus used two other metaphors to picture our roles as Christians sent into the world. "You are," he said, "the salt of the earth." "You are," he continues, "the light of the world" (Matt 5:13–14). In each case, the "locale" is the same. Earth. World. Some 3.4 billion people make up the world's workforce. Many of them belong to Jesus. Through their presence at work, they are to permeate and penetrate earth and the world as God's salty, lighted ones.

God has placed human beings as earth-rulers or earth-tenders. He wants his earth to be filled with people. All legitimate work, in some way, contributes to making earth a livable place for those people. Obeying God by taking care of his earth-business can provide a powerful motive for us to return to work day after day.

Discussion

1. In your thinking, which has seemed more obedient to God: going to church or going to work? Why?
2. Would you rate your involvement with your work as (a) engaged, (b) disengaged, or (c) actively disengaged? What evidence led you to this response?
3. How will you incorporate work-as-obedience into your work?

For more: Chapter 5 of Sherman, Doug, and William Hendricks. *Your Work Matters to God*. Colorado Springs: Navpress, 1990.

14

Close the Divide

One of my first encounters with the occupational pecking order that thrives among church people came in my early twenties. A Mothers' Day service in our church opened my eyes to this ranking system.

During that meeting, the pastor invited certain mothers to come up to the front. Not all mothers—only those whose sons or daughters were serving as pastors or missionaries. A few moms slid out of their pews and went to the platform. Most mothers remained seated. "Now," said the pastor, "we want to honor each of you for the wonderfully faithful job you did in raising your children." He then proceeded to pin an orchid on the lapel of each mother on the platform.

Seated midway back in the congregation, I suddenly felt my heart begin to race. "Wait!" I thought to myself. "This is all wrong! Where are the orchids and where is the honor for the moms who have reared solid Christian schoolteachers, truck drivers, nurses, and so on?" Those in one kind of work got honored. Those in the other kind didn't seem to count.

It took years for Tom Nelson, pastor of Christ Community Church in Leawood, Kansas, to see the Sunday-Monday disconnect. Here is an excerpt from the story he told in a video:

> About ten years into my ministry, I stood before my congregation and confessed to them . . . I'd come to the conviction that as a pastor I needed to confess my pastoral malpractice . . . For the first ten years of my ministry . . . I had failed to help people connect Sunday to Monday . . . I had failed in my pastoral vocation to equip people for all of life. In other words, I had spent the majority of my time equipping my congregation for what they were called to do in the minority of their lives. This majority-minority disparity is rampant across the pulpits of America. It is fundamental that we understand that we need to address this Sunday-to-Monday gap.[1]

Two-Tiered Thinking Has a Name

In time, I learned that this conception of work has a name: the *sacred-secular divide.* The first definition of "sacred" in the Lexico Oxford English Dictionary is: "Connected with God or a god or dedicated to a religious purpose and so deserving veneration."[2] By contrast, secular refers to anything "Not connected with religious or spiritual matters."[3]

So the sacred-secular divide means that if your paycheck comes from a church, mission, or Christian organization, then your work is sacred or spiritual. But if you're employed in an occupation not explicitly Christian, this downgrades your work to secular status.

The sacred-secular divide implies first that "sacred work" matters to God. Sacred work carries out his purposes. If you want your life's work to count for something spiritually significant, go into sacred work.

1. Nelson, "Work Matters."
2. Lexico, "Meaning of Sacred in English."
3. Lexico, "Meaning of Secular in English."

The second implication is that "secular work"—while necessary for paying the bills—doesn't really have any spiritual importance. It does, though, serve two useful roles. One, it provides a plentiful "hunting ground" in which Christians may witness to unbelievers. And two, secular work is the way Christians earn money to support those in sacred work.

Why Does This Divide Matter?

But so what? What difference does it make if we see some work as sacred and other work as secular? The difference lies in two main consequences of dividing work into these categories.

First, if we see our work as secular—not connected to God and his purposes—we will not be able to confidently present that work to him as an offering. In the Old Testament, God would not accept an inferior animal as an offering. For example, if a person were to bring "a burnt offering from the herd, you are to offer a male without defect. You must present it at the entrance to the tent of meeting so that it will be acceptable to the Lord" (Lev 1:3).

God was quite firm about having nothing substandard made into an offering. In Malachi, he asks, "When you bring injured, crippled or diseased animals and offer them as sacrifices, should I accept them from your hands?" (Mal 1:13).

We may not have known about that old covenant rule against defective offerings. And yet we new covenant believers rightly sense we should offer only the best to God. So if we have been conditioned to think of our work as sub-sacred, we won't be able to see it as something good enough to offer to God.

Second, if we see our work as secular—not connected to God and his purposes—we'll do it halfheartedly. In my theology of work course, I ask students to describe the effects of the sacred-secular divide. One of them put it like this:

> The effects are enormous; it has made Christians lazy at their work, they don't give their all since it is not a spiritual activity and cannot glorify God—so why devote time to it? We have seen work as a necessary evil that we

> will gladly get rid of if we have the autonomy, but issues of life and bills will not [allow that]. It seems those forty hours every week are a waste of our time and life because we think we are not serving God at work nor his interest.

But our regular work is not a waste of time. In his letters to the churches in Ephesus and Colossae, Paul wrote special memos to Christian slaves. These people were doing regular, everyday work—accounting, housework, engineering, farm work, government work, and so on. But Paul never distinguished between so-called "sacred" or "secular" work. Instead, he told these slaves to do their work wholeheartedly because, he said, "it is the Lord Christ you are serving" (Col 3:24).

Both Caught and Taught

Today, though, the substandard status of "secular" work comes across not only through what is said but also through what gets done in churches. Here, for example, is the unspoken message that came across from her church to a woman speaking in a video by Mark Greene:

> I teach Sunday school once a week for forty-five minutes and my church asks me to come up front so they can pray for me. For the rest of the week I'm a full-time teacher, and yet as far as I can remember, no one has ever offered to pray for the work that I do in school. It's as if they want to support half my profession and not the other half. It's difficult, because no one would say that teaching Sunday school is more important than the work I do for the rest of the week. But that sounds like the message that I get. And if you look at it this way, I've got forty-five minutes once a week with children who are generally open to the gospel with parents who are supportive of the faith, or forty-five hours a week with kids who have very little knowledge of Christianity and parents who are as ignorant of or hostile to the faith.[4]

4. Greene, "Sacred Secular Divide."

A friend of mine—I'll call her Grace—was working as a computer programmer for the US Navy. On learning of a cross-cultural mission work in Thailand, she moved there and worked more than six years for the mission. She then returned to the US and began working as a contract specialist for the federal government. Here is how she describes her experience in both places:

> Once I let Christians know I was headed for Bangkok, I suddenly began receiving frequent invitations to speak. Now that I carried the label "missionary," they just assumed I had something to say worth listening to. This surprised me, because the mission board hired me for the same skills I had been using in so-called "secular" work. Christians placed me on a pedestal because I was willing to sacrifice and suffer as a missionary. They showed keen interest in what I was doing—so long as it was called "mission work." People constantly asked how they could pray for me and my work.
>
> I was still doing the same work.

When Grace returned to work in the States, the letter-writers stopped asking about her work. The prayer support ended. "I was still doing the same things here as I had been doing there," she said. "I was still engaged in serving God full-time. But now I experienced mostly an absence of interest in my work. I felt demoted."

If they see our work as "secular," our fellow Christians won't bother to pray for it.

Spiritual Diplopia

The sacred-secular divide demeans and disables Christians. It leaves them with an ailment we might compare with diplopia—a disease of the eyes that makes a single object appear as two.

"Spiritual diplopia" occurs when daily life—including one's work—and the Christian faith are seen as two mostly separate spheres. This double vision occurs when Jesus is no longer presented as "Lord of all," including the whole of creation. Instead, he is seen as just the Lord of the "spiritual" areas. As a result, the world falsely appears as if divided into "sacred" and "secular" zones. And for far too many Christians, the workplace lands in the lower tier.

Not long after my graduation from college, I began working as an information assistant with a Washington state agency. My wife and I joined a church and became quite active in it. I was singing in the choir, teaching an adult Sunday School class, serving on a building crew, and helping out with other programs.

Feeling stretched beyond my margins, I went to the pastor and explained my dilemma. I listed all my church activities. "At the same time," I said, "I am trying to be responsible as a husband and father of two little ones. I am trying to balance the demands of home, job, and church."

He smiled and said, "Just get better organized and take on another church role." Although I was spending roughly half my waking hours in a "secular" government job, it seemed to count as a spiritual zero.

How Did Work Get Divided?

Neither in the Old Testament nor the New does Scripture even suggest that some work is "secular" in the sense that it has little or no significance to God. Adam (even before sin entered the picture) was assigned to "work" and "take care of " (Gen 2:15) the garden God himself had planted. Was his gardening/farming work secular?

Most of the godly people in the Bible had regular work that involved caring for God's earth and its people, plants, and animals. A few examples:

- Noah: boatbuilder.
- Abraham: cattleman and sheep rancher.
- Gideon: farmer, judge, military leader.
- Esther: queen in a pagan government.
- Daniel: executive in a pagan government.
- Luke: doctor.

- Cornelius: Roman military officer.
- Lydia: textile merchant.

So nothing in the Bible suggests that only church-related work counts. Instead, the sacred-secular divide has come to us through several idea-streams throughout history. Plato thought that the material world is physical, while the immaterial realm is spiritual. Gregory (pope around 600 AD) wrote, "Great are the merits of the active life, but they are surpassed by those of the contemplative life."[5]

In the eighteenth century Immanuel Kant taught a dual existence. The *noumenal* is what we can see and prove. The *phenomenal* is the invisible, spiritual dimension. In the nineteenth century, Charles Finney and other Christian revivalists pictured a two-sided reality, *spiritual* and *secular*.

Hugh Whelchel, Executive Director of the Institute for Faith, Work, & Economics, writes: "The biblical doctrine of work was all but lost to the church by the end of the nineteenth century. Finding significance in our work requires that we once again overcome the sacred-secular divide and embrace a biblical view of work."[6]

Wounded Workers

The harmful fallout from this sacred-secular divide often does not show outwardly. Some Christians work for thirty or forty years in what they have been led to believe is merely secular work. They pine for retirement when they can spend more time in church activities or short-term mission stints—the sort of work that really matters to God.

In other cases, the fallout becomes obvious for everyone to see. The following paragraphs summarize an actual situation described in a Focus on the Family website:

Tom, a young entrepreneur, created his own profitable company. As years passed, his firm earned respect in the area. Several

5. Bible Hub, "Question of the Comparison."
6. Whelchel, "Historical Influences of the Sacred-Secular Divide."

among his staff and those they served came to place their faith in Christ.

Seeing Tom's commitment, his pastor asked if he had thought about going into "full-time Christian service." The pastor's question puzzled Tom. Wasn't he already serving God every day in his business?

His pastor persisted. He acknowledged that Tom was bearing much fruit in his occupation. But, said the pastor, Tom's work was "secular." In the pastor's opinion, Tom should think about stepping up to a greater role in serving God.

A while after hearing this, Tom left his company and went overseas to work as a missionary. But as time passed, he began experiencing a number of health issues. These led him to seek help from Dr. Walt Larimore, a Christian family physician who concluded that Tom was fearful and depressed.

The doctor probed with a question. Did Tom think the work he was doing was God's will for him? Tearfully, Tom said he thought he had been doing God's will back in his previous business. Then he asked the doctor if there was such a thing as a "sacred" versus "secular" distinction in the work we do.[7]

The sacred-secular divide has handicapped not only individuals like Tom but also the church in our carrying out the mission of God in the world. The disconnection is unbiblical—as evidenced by the great number of major Bible characters whose life work was what has come to now be called "secular." This divide disheartens employees, causing them to give less than their best on the job. The same divide makes it difficult to see that the work itself is worthy of offering to God. And the idea that Christians in "secular" work should move to "something higher" can actually wound and disable them.

Clearly, we as Christians need to tell the truth about God's purposes for sending so many of his people into the work world. Only if Christians see their work as carrying God's agenda will they see the kingdom importance of what they do and the way they do it.

7. Larimore, "Employed by God."

Discussion

1. If you were to answer Tom's question about a "sacred" versus "secular" distinction in the work we do, what would you say?
2. In your own experience, what examples of the sacred-work versus secular-work divide have you encountered?
3. How might you help to eliminate the sacred-secular divide within your own sphere of influence?

For more: Chapter 6 of Overman, Christian. *God's Pleasure at Work: Bridging the Sacred-Secular Divide.* Bellevue, WA: Ablaze, 2009.

15

Become Like Christ

Expecting that God will use our work to form us spiritually provides yet another reason to get up and go to work. God used work to mature me in three stages of my own life—as a boy, young man, and senior citizen (okay, old man!).

If asked to make a sketch representing work in my boyhood years, I'd respond with two images: an asparagus knife and a hoe handle. Dad grew both asparagus and sugar beets. The first crop had to be cut and the second had to be weeded. Imagine being sent into the field to yank and cut out the weeds in ten acres of sugar beets. As I surveyed the field—the size of 7.5 football fields—I suspected it held a million weeds. And the rows of beets seemed endless.

So I started at the beginning of row one. Then it was weed after weed after weed. Scotch thistle, morning glory, prickly lettuce, nightshade, and on and on, row after row. At the end of the first day, I could look back on a number of (I hoped) weed-free rows. Then it was day two, three, four, and so on. What was God forming in me spiritually? A quality that Jesus had: *persistence* and *endurance*. Staying at the job until I could say, as he had said about his work, "It is finished."

Fast forward now to my young-man years. I was working as an editor/writer for a Sunday School take-home paper. I would often interview Christians and write up their stories. Each article usually ran about 1500 words. I poured my heart into each piece. Saw it as a masterpiece when complete.

Then my boss, with his red pencil, took over. One time, after his editorial surgery, I counted words. Six hundred were left from my original draft; nine hundred words came from the boss. What kind of spiritual formation was taking place in me? Again, a Jesus-attribute: *humility*. Jesus humbled himself. I could not humble myself by myself. God used my work to do it.

Now to the present, senior-citizen, stage. For the last eight years I have taught the theology of work for graduate students online. My classes have included people from Vietnam, Singapore, Guatemala, Brazil, Canada, Jamaica, Ethiopia, Ghana, Nigeria, the US, and many other nations.

In this phase of my work life, I have seen God expanding something else in me: *kingdom vision*. Through my work, God has enlarged my perspective, my appreciation for other theological insights, other ethnic groups, and other cultures. My kingdom vision still falls far short of what Jesus sees, but it's growing—and doing so through my work.

Spiritual formation at every stage has involved growing pains. New growth rings never came easily. But in every life chapter, the gains have been worth the pains. So here's another reason God loves your work: *He uses it to form Christ in you.*

Work Becomes an Altar

I had gone to work in the information office of the Washington State Department of Highways. My role? I served as the editor of the magazine called *Washington State Highways*. As an energetic twenty-six-year-old, I was bursting with article ideas for the magazine. But whenever I went into his office to propose a story to my boss, he consistently shot it down. Time after time after time. Frustration began to build up inside me.

On the side, on my own time, I began working on a "parachute," a project that would, I hoped, make it possible for me to bail out of the state job. But down below my urge to flee, I began to hear God's still small voice saying, "stay." Finally, the pressure grew so intense that I went into my little office at home, shut the door, and went face-down on the floor before God. I handed over to him my wife, my kids, my house, my income, my future—in a nutshell, my whole life.

Looking back now, I recognize all this as spiritual formation. What means had God used to bring it about? In this case, his tool of choice was my so-called "secular" job. My work became an altar on which he was calling me to lay down my life.

"God has made us so that through working we actually sculpt the kind of selves we each are becoming, in time and for eternity."[1] That's what Lester DeKoster says in his book, *Work: The Meaning of Your Life*. In other words, he is saying that just a sculptor's chisel shapes stone, our work carves our character.

How Work Shapes Character

Does this surprise you? As Christians, most of us might think of sermons, Bible studies, and prayer meetings as God's instruments for helping shape us into the likeness of his Son. All these activities seem surrounded by a kind of churchy, stained-glass aura. But our daily work? How could anything so gritty and earthy bring about spiritual change?

Jesus often used objects in what we call the natural world to teach us spiritual lessons. So let's begin with an illustration that's probably been overused. How do diamonds form deep in the earth? They develop under great heat and extreme pressure. Surrounded by all this intensity, carbon atoms crystallize and change into diamonds. It seems that it takes analogous conditions to form spiritual "diamonds" in the human heart.

1. De Koster, *Work: The Meaning of Your Life*, 9.

What words do we often associate with jobs in the world of work? Stress. Pressure. Heat. Tension. Hassle. Yes, we also use such words to describe pain we encounter in off-the-job relationships and activities. But at work, this unrelenting strain stretches on hour after hour, day after day, year after year.

We spend, perhaps, the single largest block of our waking hours in the workplace. And it is there that we encounter toxic coworkers. Impatient bosses. You've-got-to-be-kidding deadlines. Untimely equipment breakdowns. Unyielding obstacles. Irate customers, students, patients, vendors, and so on. Stress. Pressure. Heat.

Work as Cross-Bearing

Tough duty? Yes. But God leaves no doubt: work is to occupy a major part of our waking hours. In Exodus 20:9 God says we are to work six days—six days out of seven. Nothing in the New Testament changes that original assignment to work on an essentially daily basis.

But the New Testament does tell us something else we're to do daily. "If anyone would come after me," Jesus says, "he must deny himself and take up his cross daily and follow me." I think you'll agree that daily cross-bearing and following Jesus lie at the very heart of spiritual formation. The equation works like this:

WORKING 86 percent of our days,

PLUS taking up our cross 100 percent of our days,

EQUALS the bulk of spiritual formation must take place in the context of our work.

Workplace spiritual formation happened back in Bible days. In David's first job, he served as a sheepherder for his father, Jesse. Working far from city tensions may seem to us like stress-free work. But David had to deal with wild animals bent on having mutton for dinner.

One day his dad sent David to check on his older brothers who were off with King Saul fighting against the Philistines. David arrived just as the nine-foot giant, Goliath, was striking terror into the hearts of the whole Israelite army. Appalled that this pagan was defying the army of the true God, David offered to go and fight him. No way, the king said, "You're only a boy."

But David told Saul, "Your servant has been keeping his father's sheep. When a lion or bear came and carried off one of the sheep from the flock I went after it, struck it, and rescued the sheep from its mouth. When it turned on me, I seized it by its hair, struck and killed it. Your servant has killed both the lion and the bear . . . The Lord who delivered me the lion and the bear will deliver me from the hand of this Philistine" (1 Sam 17:33–37). We all know what happened next.

But think about the spiritual formation David had experienced in his shepherding work and how that prepared him to take on the giant. Guarding the sheep had brought him up against terrifying circumstances. When the lion came, he must have been tempted to run for his life. When the bear confronted him with its powerful jaws and claws, David's adrenaline surely spiked. In each case he had trusted God to intervene—and God did so. Thanks to on-the-job spiritual formation, David was ready to trust God to see him through an even larger challenge.

David could have turned tail and fled when the lion and bear threatened his father's sheep. But he didn't. He chose to stay put, to trust God, and to take his stand. Those workplace experiences strengthened him to make the same kind of faith-choice when facing Goliath and later when serving as king.

Lester DeKoster underscores the importance of the choices we make on the job: "How do we sculpt ourselves on the job? We do it with the chisel of choice, day by day. How well do we choose to do the work at hand? How well do we choose to develop and use the talents God has given us? What is the quantity and the quality of the work we choose to turn out, every hour? How do we choose—as employer or employee—to relate to others on the job?"[2]

2. DeKoster, *Work: The Meaning of Your Life*, 22.

Workplace: the *Primary* Location for Spiritual Formation?

What about Jesus? Yes, he was and is God. But he was and is also fully human. What kinds of choices did he make as he worked in the family carpentry or construction business? Scripture is silent on that. But we do know something about the choices he made working under his capital-F Father in the "workshop" of his public life and ministry.

We know that when it came to the most difficult work of giving his life for us on the cross, he chose not to do his own will but to do the will of his Father. And the writer of Hebrews tells us, "Son though he was, he learned obedience from what he suffered" (Heb 5:8). Sinless, yes. But even the man Jesus was formed spiritually—learned lessons of obedience—under pressures and stresses.

Eugene Peterson, perhaps best known for *The Message* paraphrase of the Bible, wrote many other books. In *Christ Plays in Ten Thousand Places*, he says:

> Every Christian man or woman who gets out of bed and goes to work walks into a world in which idolatry is the major temptation for seducing him or her away from the new life of being formed by resurrection into the likeness of Christ . . . Most of us spend a lot of time at work. This means that our Christian identity is being formed much of the time under uncongenial if not downright hostile conditions . . . That is why Christian formation demands endless vigilance.[3]

Then he adds: "I'm prepared to contend that the primary location for spiritual formation is the workplace." Notice, Peterson did not call work *a* primary location but *the* primary location that forms us spiritually. How might Peterson's statement change the way you view your own work?

3. Peterson, *Christ Plays in Ten Thousand Places*, 127.

Discussion

1. What are the pressures, frustrations, stresses, or dilemmas that you are encountering in connection with your work?
2. How have you, as a Christian, grown through workplace worries and hassles?
3. In what ways do Jesus' words about taking up our cross and following him apply in the world of your work?

For more: Chapters 2–3 of DeKoster, Lester. *Work: The Meaning of Your Life*. Grand Rapids, MI: Christian's Library, 1982.

16

Watch How I Work

Growing up on a small farm, I learned early to work hard. Dad paid me by the hour. For cutting asparagus, I—like the other high-schoolers on the crew—received ninety cents an hour. With a conscience trained by my hard-working father, I knew better than to slack off while on the clock.

That's what made my first job away from home so astonishing. At eighteen years old, I traveled the two thousand miles from our farm to college in Wheaton, Illinois, where I enrolled as a freshman. With no rich uncle to pay my way, I found a job right away. As mentioned in chapter 6, I went to work as janitor of the third-floor of a junior-high school. After the first week or two, emptying wastebaskets, cleaning erasers, and straightening desks became routine. I began discovering time-saving shortcuts.

By the end of my first month or so of janitoring, the school principal asked me to stop by his office. At eighteen, I still had some residual discomfort at being summoned to the principal's office. "Is there a problem with my work?" I asked him. "No—you're going a great job," he said with a broad smile. "It's just that you're reporting far fewer hours on your time sheet than the janitors on floors one and two. They say you're making them look bad. Why not just mark down more hours?"

Definitely not what I had expected to hear! His advice was appealing. But as I pondered doing what the principal had suggested, I knew I would never feel right about just dawdling on the job or lying about the hours I had actually worked. So before long, I found another job—at McDonald's.

The Need for Workplace Ethics

That temptation to over-report hours worked was my introduction to the whole area of workplace ethics. Back then, of course, I had no idea what an immense ethical challenge exists in the world of work. The list of unethical behaviors on the job is long. Here are just a few examples:

- Not reporting unethical behavior by others.
- Using employer-paid time for personal purposes.
- Putting down the boss behind his or her back.
- Slacking off when the boss is nowhere in sight.
- Gossiping about coworkers.
- Taking credit for the work done by others.
- Not following organizational procedures.

Wrongdoing costs employers plenty. Some estimates say that, globally, employers are losing $2.9 trillion each year as a result of employee fraud and theft.[1] And in the US, it is estimated that about one-third of company bankruptcies occur as a result of thieving employees.[2]

In its 2020 "Report to the Nations," the Association of Certified Fraud Examiners (ACFE) details the results of its study

1. Simmons, "Mad as Hell and Stealing from Employers."
2. Zuckerman, "39 Employee Theft Statistics."

of 2,504 cases in 125 nations. These cases totaled $3.6 billion in losses. The report says:

- Certain fraud risks were more likely in small businesses than in large organizations.
- Men committed 72 percent of all occupational fraud and also caused larger losses than women.
- The typical fraud case lasts fourteen months before detection and causes a loss of $8,300 per month.
- The US Equal Employment Opportunity Commission (EEOC) reports that it received more than 7,500 claims of sexual harassment in 2019. More than 82 percent of these allegations were made by females. The monetary benefits paid for claims found to be valid: $68.2 million.[3]

Employees shortchange employers in other ways as well. Gallup polls consistently find that nearly two-thirds of employees are either "not engaged" or "actively disengaged" from their work.[4]

Ethical Lapses among Christians

Lack of engagement may be even worse among Christian workers. In his book *Good Work*, David Hataj says, "A common complaint I hear from Christian executives is that their employees don't 'get into' their work, so busy and motivated are they with church activities and Bible studies."[5]

"Today's corporate world is lost in work's ethical wilderness."[6] With that statement, Norman L. Geisler and Randy Douglass open chapter 1 in their book, *Integrity at Work*. They cite a survey of three hundred respondents that asked Christian employees to name ethical issues they encounter on the job. Those responding

3. ACFE, "2020 Global Fraud Study."
4. Harter, "US Employee Engagement Rises Following Wild 2020."
5. Hataj, *Good Work*, 11.
6. Geisler and Douglass, *Integrity at Work*, 13.

listed everything from dishonesty (40 percent), to sexual pressures (44 percent) to cheating (30 percent)—to name only a few. When asked if they felt they handled these situations well, a full 74 percent said no.[7]

Workplace Ethics in the Bible

Ethical decisions in the workplace are nothing new. Bible characters faced a great variety of such choices in their places of work. It all began in the Garden of Eden—a workplace.

Adam had an assignment to "work it [the garden] and take care of it" (Gen 2:15). And it was in that work environment that our first foreparents made their world-shattering ethical choice about the forbidden fruit.

Cain brought God an unacceptable offering from the fruit of his labor. He then deceptively invited his brother into his field, his workplace. The murder that took place there launched what we now call workplace violence.

Laban entered into one of the world's first labor contracts. He said to Jacob, "Name your wages, and I will pay them." Jacob asked for only one provision in their contract: "Let me go through all your flocks today and remove from them every speckled or spotted sheep, every dark-colored lamb and every spotted or speckled goat. They will be my wages" (Gen 30:32). Laban agreed—then sneakily removed all the spotted and speckled animals and made himself scarce.

Later, Jacob told his wives—Laban's daughters—"You know that I've worked for your father with all my strength, yet your father has cheated me by changing my wages ten times" (Gen 31:6–7). So much for honoring a labor contract!

Moses saw an injustice in the workplace of his Israelite kinfolk—an Egyptian beating a Hebrew slave. As Prince Moses, with all kinds of influence with the pharaoh, he could have reported this to

7. Geisler and Douglass, *Integrity at Work*, 17.

the palace and possibly have made a difference. Instead, he looked both ways, murdered the Egyptian, and tried to hide his crime.

Boaz, the farmer, made an ethical decision concerning his crops. Shall I tell my harvesters to take everything—to strip the field clean? Or shall I order them to leave some barley stocks for Ruth to glean? He made the ethically right choice.

Nehemiah—Shall I ignore the violations of the covenant with God? Or shall I rebuke the violators and call them to account? Nehemiah, too, chose the right course of action.

Daniel—Shall I eat the King's food and violate my conscience? Or shall I seek a way that does not involve compromise? Daniel and his fellow Israelites did the right thing.

Biblical Ethics for the Workplace

Many Scripture passages describe the ethical behavior God expects us to practice. *The Message* paraphrase makes the following examples vivid:

- "Sloth makes you poor; diligence brings wealth" (Prov 10:4).
- "A lazy employee will give you nothing but trouble; it's vinegar in the mouth, smoke in the eyes" (Prov 10:26).
- "God hates cheating in the marketplace; he loves it when business is aboveboard" (Prov 11:1).
- "Slack habits and sloppy work are as bad as vandalism" (Prov 18:9).
- "The sullen servant who does shoddy work will be held responsible. Being Christian doesn't cover up bad work" (Col 3:25).
- "Don't you remember the rule we had when we lived with you? 'If you don't work, you don't eat'" (2 Thess 3:10).

Typically, a workplace will put us into a relationship with non-Christians. Philippians 2:15 and 1 Peter 2:12 speak specifically to our conduct among people who are not following Christ.

"Live clean, innocent lives as children of God, shining like bright lights in a world full of crooked and perverse people" (Phil 2:15, NLT).

"Be careful to live properly among your unbelieving neighbors. Then even if they accuse you of doing wrong, they will see your honorable behavior, and they will give honor to God when he judges the world" (1 Pet 2:12, NLT). These verses show us (a) our calling, (b) our context, and (c) our conduct.

- Our calling: we are "children of God."
- Our context: "a world full of crooked and perverse people"; "unbelieving neighbors"; "they accuse you of doing wrong."
- Our conduct: "live clean, innocent lives"; "shining like bright lights"; "live properly;" "honorable behavior."

An Ethical Decision-Making Process

Given the issues and often-perplexing choices in the context of today's world of work, how can we—when faced with an ethical issue—decide what to do? Sometimes we will need to make an instant judgment call right away on what to do.

But if we have time to reflect on the matter before us, the following series of seven steps may help. To illustrate how these steps work, we'll trace the decision Joseph had to make when he was being sexually harassed.

1. *Pray: How can you—alone or with others—ask God for wisdom on this issue?*

Joseph undoubtedly had time to pray when he was being propositioned by Potiphar's wife. "Day after day" she was saying, "Come to bed with me" (Gen 39:6, 10). As the wife of the king's captain of the guard, she clearly held the power position in this case of sexual harassment.

2. *Collect the Facts: What are the relevant circumstances or background events?*

In Joseph's case, the ingredients of the situation set the stage for some potentially serious immoral behavior. A handsome, well-built young man, far away from all the accountability structures of home. A rich, bored wife with far too much time on her hands.

3. *Describe the Issue: What is the ethical dilemma? Right/wrong? Fair/unfair?*

The situation Joseph faced was basically a choice between morality vs. immorality. He could either ignore or honor the marriage covenant between Potiphar and his wife.

4. *Identify the Standards: Biblical principles/instructions? Organizational policies? Government laws?*

At creation, God established marriage between one man and one woman. Even pagans recognized any violation of the marriage covenant as sin (Gen 26:10).

5. *Note Possible Responses: What action choices are available?*

Joseph could choose to: (a) comply with the woman's repeated urgings, (b) try to argue her out of her demands, or (c) exit immediately.

6. *Project the Outcomes: Who will be helped or harmed? What would be the effects on conscience, character, or environment?*

For Joseph, indulgence would mean lies, secrecy, revenge, and a corrupted character. His refusal would mean integrity preserved, probable false accusation, and possible imprisonment.

7. Decide and Follow Through: What do you intend to do? When will you act?

Joseph decided: Flee! Now!

Gray Areas

Some ethical decisions in the workplace are not clear-cut, good-versus-bad decisions. Read the following case study as if you were the business owner. What would you do?

> *You own and operate a small pizza restaurant. Before the COVID-19 pandemic, you employed twenty-three people. During a government-mandated shutdown, you shift to nothing but takeout orders. This means you are able to retain only seven employees on the payroll. Although the other sixteen begin receiving unemployment benefits, you assure them you will hold their jobs for them once the government permits you to open your doors again.*
>
> *After the governor of your state allows restaurants to do so, you reopen for dine-in customers. You are carefully complying with all the safety requirements—disinfecting surfaces, placing tables at least six feet apart, testing employee health, and so on. Business is quickly returning to near what had been normal. When you contact all of your laid-off employees and invite them to report to work, seven return. However, nine, fearful of contracting the virus, refuse to come back. Yet they insist that you hold their positions open for them until they feel safe to return. All told, the nine unwilling to work are the primary breadwinners for their households, including three single moms.*
>
> *The fresh surge of customers means you cannot stay open with a crew short by nine employees. Closing the business would put the other fourteen—those who have returned—out of work. Several qualified people seeking work have applied for positions.*

What action will you take?

Discussion

1. Describe an ethical workplace decisions you have made. What was the situation? What did you decide to do—and why?
2. Do you think the "Ethical Decision-Making Process" given in this chapter will be useful? Why or why not?
3. After reading the case study of the pizza restaurant, what would you do if you owned the place?

For more: Chapter 1 of Gill, David. *Doing Right: Practicing Ethical Principles*. Downers Grove, IL: InterVarsity, 2004.

17

Caution: Money at Work

When he learned that he had been chosen for the job, Charlie could hardly believe the good news. His employer, Bentley Morgan, had made his fortune in the stock market. Now a multimillionaire, he was making even more money through loans to startup businesses. Out of a dozen prospects, Morgan had selected Charlie to manage his loans.

At first, everything went well. Charlie kept all the accounts current, with loan-repayment installments coming in like clockwork. But as time passed, Charlie learned how to deal with all the creditors and the job lost its urgency for him. Increasingly, clients missed payment deadlines, and two even defaulted. Seeing the falling bottom line, Bentley Morgan grew more and more testy—and finally became furious.

One day he ordered Charlie into his office. Even before he sat down, Charlie could read the message written all over Morgan's face. Staring out the window, Morgan began ticking off the late and undersized loan payments. Finally, he whirled around, looked directly at Charlie, and said, "Consider this your two-week notice."

Even as he was leaving Morgan's office, Charlie began mentally assembling his exit plan. Maybe he could up his chances for future employment elsewhere. That afternoon, he got on the phone to creditor A: "How much do you owe Bentley Morgan? $500,000? Okay, pay $250,000 within a week and we'll cancel your debt." Next call went to creditor B. Same question. "One million dollars? If you'll write check for $400,000 within the next seven days, you'll be free and clear."

Do you recognize this story? It's an updated retelling of the parable Jesus tells in Luke 16, often called "the story of the shrewd manager." In that narrative, the boss praises the just-fired manager for being shrewd. Clearly, what that ex-manager did would assure him of some friendly faces among those creditors / potential employers. Jesus follows this parable with three points.

1. "Use worldly wealth to gain friends for yourselves, so that when it is gone, you will be welcomed into eternal dwellings" (16:9). Bible scholars don't agree on what the "eternal dwellings" part may mean. But I think Jesus is saying at least this: *When you're handling money, be as sharp and forward-looking as that discharged manager.*
2. "If you have not been trustworthy with someone else's property, who will give you property of your own?" (16:12). *God has entrusted you with a certain income—but remember, it all belongs to him.*
3. "You cannot serve both God and money" (16:13). *You can serve either God or money—choose one.*

Let's pause for a closer look at those three points, one at a time.

First, When You're Handling Money, Be as Sharp and Forward-Looking as That Discharged Manager.

In *The Spirit of the Disciplines*, Dallas Willard says Christians "are troubled by the idea that the very possession of surplus goods or money is evil."[1] Willard then helpfully defines three relationships

1. Willard, *Spirit of the Disciplines*, 193.

to money. We can (a) possess it, (b) use it, or (c) trust in it. Understanding these will help us be shrewd money-managers.

Possessing Money. It may ease our minds to realize that even Jesus and his disciples possessed money. They kept a money supply to navigate in their first-century society. Of Judas we read, "as keeper of the money bag, he used to help himself to what was put into it" (John 12:6). If Judas could dip into the bag from time to time, Jesus and his disciples must have kept a standing balance.

Since Jesus and his disciples did not work in paying jobs, where did they get their funds? They apparently had an income from "women [who] were helping to support them out of their own means" (Luke 8:3). So we should abandon any notion that having money is wrong.

Using Money. Possessing money gives us the say-so over how it will be spent. We may use it this way or that way. We may use it to keep ourselves from being dependent on others. We may use it for the benefit of those in need. Or we may use it to gratify our own selfish wishes. Using money, then, can either further God's will being done on earth—or not.

Using money means we have control over the purposes to which it will be put. Let's say you have a sum of money you believe you should give to someone. But as you think and pray about doing so, you feel uneasy. Giving the money to that particular person would mean they would both possess and use it. Their lifestyle and spending habits, though, persuade you that they would misuse it, spending it in ways out of line with God's kingdom purposes. So long as you possess those dollars, with control over how they will be used, you can prevent any such misuse.

Trusting Money. We are tempted to trust money as the means of getting something we prize. Maybe we lean on money for security—amassing wealth to guarantee we will be fed, clothed, and housed in the future. Perhaps we depend on money for shopping sprees—heaping up stuff we think will make us happy. Or maybe we count on money for self-worth, measuring our value by the size of our bank account in comparison with others.

Jesus spoke about the "deceitfulness of wealth" (Mark 4:19). Buying into its lie and trusting money turns it into an idol. This helps explain why the love of money is the root of all evil. "Whoever trusts in his riches will fall" (Prov 11:28).

Second, God Has Entrusted You with a Certain Income—but Remember, It All Belongs to Him.

It's time for your semiannual visit to the dentist. Once you're settled in the dental chair, the hygienist says this time you need X-rays. Then she covers the upper part of your body with a blanket that feels like it's lined with lead (and it is). She asks you to open your mouth. As you do, she pushes an irritating apparatus between your molars. "Now bite down on it," she says. Once that's in place, she disappears behind a wall. You hear a tiny buzz-beep sound, and she returns to remove both the framework and the heavy vest.

Why the lead blanket? And why did she go behind the wall? To shield both of you from being harmed by the X-rays. Although the radiation from that X-ray machine is miniscule, too much of it in repeated doses can lead to cancer and other unwanted effects.

Working in the marketplace exposes you to money. And just as X-rays can damage us physically, money can injure us spiritually. Money, then, is an occupational hazard. For all of us it takes money to live in this world—our own or funds that belong to someone else. At the same time, a wage or salary lays us open to temptation. Your name on the paycheck makes it appear as if you own the money. That's part of the "deceitfulness of riches" Jesus speaks about.

In his book *How the Church Fails Businesspeople*, John C. Knapp says:

> The church has never quite found a consensus on how to reconcile the biblical injunctions to give thanks to God for wealth and also to renounce any desire for it. This ambivalence widens the chasm between the worlds of

> faith and work, for the subject of work cannot be fully addressed apart from the making and spending of money.[2]

The chasm he refers to runs right through the Bible. It sends us two messages about money that seem at odds with each other. For instance:

- On the one hand, it affirms money as a gift from God: "Remember the Lord your God, for it is he who gives you the ability to produce wealth" (Deut 8:18).
- On the other hand, it gives us an either/or: "No one can serve two masters. Either he will hate the one and love the other, or he will be devoted to the one and despise the other. You cannot serve both God and Money" (Matt 6:24).
- Then again, money is a favor from God: "The blessing of the Lord brings wealth, and he adds no trouble to it" (Prov 10:22).
- And yet, Jesus tells a young man, "Sell everything you have and give to the poor, and you will have treasure in heaven. Then come, follow me" (Luke 18:22).

It's those verses and others like them that give us pause about money, right?

Jesus told the wealthy ruler to sell off everything he owned and to donate it all to the poor. The young man was wealthy. His money had a grip on him—a grip he could not break. He did not realize that he was only a manager of money that belonged to God.

Third, You Can Serve Either God or Money—Choose One.

The X-ray metaphor (above) can illustrate the *destructive* power of money. But a magnet may better suggest the *drawing* power of money. I have seen photos of hospital beds, office chairs, and wheelchairs being sucked into the mouths of magnetic resonance imaging (MRI) machines. In a similar way, the invisible but potent attraction of money can pull us away from serving God as Master

2. Knapp, *How the Church Fails Businesspeople*, 67.

and put money in his place. "Those who want to get rich fall into temptation and a trap and into many foolish and harmful desires that plunge people into ruin and destruction" (1 Tim 6:9–10).

Unplugging it can disable the power of an MRI machine. But what can cut the pulling power of money? Resolutions and rules cannot cancel out the seductive appeal of wealth. No, pulling the plug on the money magnet requires something far more drastic.

Jesus says, "Whoever wants to be my disciple must deny themselves and take up their cross daily and follow me" (Luke 9:23). A cross means death. Following Jesus means following him that far. Jesus took up his cross, so following him requires taking up ours—traveling the same path he took. Of course, our sin-infested human nature refuses to go there.

But as Christ followers, we can count on something far stronger than our flesh. As Paul puts it, "I have been crucified with Christ and I no longer live, but Christ lives in me" (Gal 2:20). The Christ who lives in us has already made the journey down into death and come up in resurrection life. United with him by faith, we inherit his trek through death and back into life.

That co-death with Christ continues as a sin-killing force in us. As Paul puts it, "We always carry around in our body the death of Jesus, so that the life of Jesus may also be revealed in our body. For we who are alive are always being given over to death for Jesus' sake, so that his life may be revealed in our mortal body. So then, death is at work in us, but life is at work in you" (2 Cor 4:10–12).

Counting on his "death at work in us," we are able to "put to death . . . greed, which is idolatry" (Col 3:5). This is the way to deal with the powerful and deceptive pull of money. But, as Jesus says, this taking up of his cross must happen "daily." Once a week on Sundays won't work.

Reorienting Two Money-Related Church Words

As we continue to work, money keeps coming our way. It may help us deal with it if we revisit the way we think about two words in our church vocabulary.

Offering. Taking up our cross each day will make us able to offer not only the work itself but also the money that comes to us through it. Long-time Christians know about "the offering" in our gathered churches. Once we've deposited some money in "the offering," it is all too easy to think of what's left as our own.

Out in the scattered church, we may find it difficult to apply to money the concept of "offering." In that context, there is no offering plate or box. So—given the magnetic pull of what arrives in each paycheck—we need to remind ourselves that it all belongs to God.

Knowing this all-too-human focus on self, Moses told the Israelites: "If you start thinking to yourselves, 'I did all this. And all by myself. I'm rich. It's all mine!'—well, think again. Remember that God, your God, gave you the strength to produce all this wealth" (Deut 8:17–18, MSG). Anything we earn comes from God, the earnings rightfully belong to him. We are simply his money-managers.

Stewardship. In the gathered church, we've learned to think of stewardship Sunday and stewardship campaigns. Such terms can lead us to relate "stewardship" to certain days and special emphases. We respond to calls to give money to meet some need or to fund a building program. But "stewardship" covers far more.

A steward is a property manager—someone who looks after, say, a house while the owner is away. The state of being a steward is steward*ship*. As God's stewards, we are to be shrewd as we care for his property: our own bodies, our families, our jobs—and our money.

Money? Salaries? Wages? Yes, they pose a threat to us spiritually. Living in this world in its present form confronts us with all kinds of physical risks. Driving a car exposes us to danger. So does flying in a plane. Yet we take the proper precautions and still travel by highway and air. In a similar way, staying alert and with great care, we can use money, because in Christ God has given us the arsenal we need to deal with it wisely in ways that prevent it from ruining us.

Discussion

1. In what area do you most need to grow in stewarding the money God has entrusted to you?
2. How do you understand taking up your cross daily as it relates to using money?
3. How do you reconcile the seemingly opposite positions on money found in the Bible?

For more: Chapter 10 of Willard, Dallas. *The Spirit of the Disciplines: Understanding How God Changes Lives.* New York: HarperOne, 2001.

18

Support Yourself and Your Family

PAYING YOUR OWN AND your family's way may seem like an obvious reason to get up and go to work. After all, don't most people work for money to cover the bills? While that is probably true, for many of us who follow Jesus the money issue leaves us a bit unsettled.

Dallas Willard, in *The Spirit of the Disciplines*, recognizes this anxiety. "Possessions and money," he writes, "cause uneasiness today in the minds of many sincere Christians. It is not just that they fear failing in their clear responsibilities to help others with the goods at their disposal. Rather, then are haunted by the more radical thought that their service to God would be better if they were poor—or at least if they owned nothing beyond what is required to meet their day-to-day needs."[1]

The Money Maze

Part of our uneasiness stems from the fact that the Bible seems to say one thing about money here and something else there. Abraham was wealthy. The widow who dropped her coin into the temple treasury was poor. On the one hand: "But remember the

1. Willard, *Spirit of the Disciplines*, 193.

Lord your God, for it is he who gives you the ability to produce wealth" (Deut 8:18). Yet on the other hand: "Those who want to get rich fall into temptation and a trap and into many foolish and harmful desires that plunge people into ruin and destruction" (1 Tim 6:9).

For a great many Christians, the whole business of working for money seems tainted. For this reason, some choose to work for a nonprofit rather than a for-profit organization. Those familiar with the King James translation of the Bible recall that "ye cannot serve God and mammon" (Matt 6:24). The same translation warns against "filthy lucre" (1 Tim 3:3). Described in those terms, money seems like a substance that carries something contagious, a nasty virus we'd best run from.

In his *Christianity Today* article "Modern Voices: The Christian and Money," Randy Petersen writes: "The various Christian theories about money raise a confusing cacophony, differing on basic biblical interpretation and fundamental views of human society."[2] He lists and describes eight distinct ways serious Christians look at money.

What to think about and to do with money can bewilder anyone who sincerely wants to please God. Should one of our reasons for working be to earn money to spend on ourselves and our families? Or does doing that smack of self-centeredness?

The Family Man Who Turned Down a Job

Just after college graduation, I worked for a company that published Christian educational materials. Because the company served churches in the US and other countries, it employed quite a number of people in its warehouse and distribution center. One day the leaders in that firm learned that a professing Christian, a man with a wife and several children, desperately needed work. So they offered him a job in the shipping department.

2. Petersen, "Modern Voices: The Christian and Money."

But the man refused. He was dead-set on finding work as a corporate executive. He sat around at home all day wearing a suit and tie—literally acting out the big-shot role he dreamed of filling. Day after day he waited for the phone to ring with an offer of his ideal job. Despite repeated efforts by several, he could not be persuaded to take the shipping-room position. He saw that kind of work as beneath him.

Meanwhile, because his family was going hungry, several of us took turns purchasing and delivering bagsful of groceries to the man's wife. She and the kids had to eat, even if husband and father continued to snub a paying job.

A Stern Word for Non-Supporters

God does not take lightly this kind of family neglect. When Timothy went to Ephesus, he had to deal with various out-of-line issues among the believers in the church there. Paul sent him a letter with instructions on handling these situations. One of them paralleled the case of the man just described.

In 1 Timothy 5:8, Paul wrote, "Anyone who does not provide for their relatives, and especially for their own household, has denied the faith and is worse than an unbeliever." *The Message* paraphrase puts it even more vividly: "Anyone who neglects to care for family members in need repudiates the faith. That's worse than refusing to believe in the first place."

Why would Paul say that Christians who won't support their own families are "worse" than unbelievers? That sounds so harsh. Certainly failure to provide displeases God. But how does such negligence put a professing Christian in that worse-than category?

None of us can read Paul's mind on his reason for such a hard statement. But I suspect he may have had at least two things in mind.

First, a great many who do not follow Jesus consistently support their families financially. You probably have non-Christian neighbors who work hard to keep their families housed, fed, and clothed. What explains this right behavior? Natural law. It's what Paul described when he wrote, "the requirements of the law are written on their [gentiles'] hearts" (Rom 2:15). So Christians whose faith commits them to carry out the "law of Christ" but refuse to live even by this universally recognized natural law concerning family are worse than unbelievers.

Second, one of the names of the God we Christians worship is *Jehovah-Jireh*—"the Lord is our Provider." God the Father gave his Son. His Son gave his life. Each one of us is made in the image of this generous, self-giving God. If we claim to know this God yet refuse to support financially those who rightfully look to us to do so, the hypocrisy makes us worse than unbelievers.

Who Makes Up Your "Household"?

First Timothy 5:8 calls for providing for one's own "household." That word, in the Greek original, includes those we call "immediate family" but can stretch to take in others as well. So your household consists of all those for whom you have a responsibility to provide. Put that way, who might your household include?

Yourself

Providing for your own needs is not self-centered. It is an obedient response to God. If you are able-bodied, freeloading from others is not an option. The work of a man, a woman, or both may bring in the income.

Spouse

In a marriage, even if one stays home to care for the chores and any children, his or her work—even though unpaid—counts as part of the provision. That spouse also has a right to be supported from the income of the working-for-pay person.

Natural Children

Children have a God-given right to parental support. When writing to assure the Corinthian Christians he is not after their money, Paul writes: "Children should not have to save up for their parents, but parents for their children" (2 Cor 12:14).

Adopted Children

Any adopted kids have the same right to support as natural children.

Parents

As our parents age, they often become dependent again. In many families, the parents of the providers are to be seen as part of the household.

Others

Circumstances often lead to arrangements in which outsiders become insiders. In this way they also become those who deserve financial support as part of the household.

To Save or Not to Save?

As a young adult, I heard all sorts of advice about saving and investing money to meet future needs. Again and again others explained the power of compound interest to build a nest egg and a rainy day fund. But I resisted all such advice.

Why? Because I took seriously Jesus' words in Matthew 6:19–21: "Do not store up for yourselves treasures on earth, where moths and vermin destroy, and where thieves break in and steal. But store up for yourselves treasures in heaven, where moths and vermin do not destroy, and where thieves do not break in and steal. For where your treasure is, there your heart will be also." And I absolutely did not want my heart getting pinned down by earthly treasure.

Starting in my mid-twenties, I worked eleven years for a government agency which took money from my paycheck, matched it, and deposited it into a pension fund. During those years someone else put money away for me—I had no choice in the matter. So I could still say that I was not the one storing up treasure for myself.

At the end of those eleven years, my government days ended. Now I was out there with a business of my own and a growing family. As time passed and I watched my parents approach their non-earning years, I began to reconsider my application of Jesus' words. For example, I read what the book of Proverbs says about the ways and wisdom of the ant—the little insect that stores up its food in summer (Prov 6:8).

What Paul said in his instructions to the church in Thessalonica also caused me to rethink my earlier stance: "You should mind your own business and work with your hands, just as we told you, so that your daily life may win the respect of outsiders and so that you will not be dependent on anybody" (1 Thess 4:11–12).

A few Christians I knew had reached their retirement years without having given any serious attention to putting anything away. They had to lean on others for support—quite contrary to Paul's call to "not be dependent on anybody." Learning from their example, I finally began to invest a portion of my income from the business to meet future needs.

We now live in a community for seniors. And because we began putting money aside, anticipating our non-income years, we do not need to depend on our children or others to pay our way. Sometimes, of course, circumstances such as poor health or a dried-up job market make it impossible to follow the example of the ant.

Including Family in Your Work

Income from work can support a family financially. But supporting your family through your work might also mean involving them in what you do there. Sometimes, this proves to be difficult. In 2016, baseball star Adam LaRoche made headlines when he walked away from a $13-million-a-year contract. He did so because the Chicago White Sox asked him to stop bringing his son, Drake, so often to team practices and its clubhouse.

Getting kids involved in the work of their parents—while fairly rare today—has a lot of historical precedent. The Jewish rabbis had a proverb: "He who does not teach his son a trade, teaches him to be a thief." Paul probably learned tentmaking as he worked alongside his father. The New Testament tells us that both Joseph and Jesus worked as carpenters or builders (Matt 13:55, Mark 6:3). They must have spent many hours together on various projects.

Self-employment makes it easier to spend time working with kids and finding useful tasks for them to perform. Growing up on a farm, I put in many hours beside my dad. We replaced the piston rings in the John Deere every winter. As a member of his asparagus-cutting crew, he and I worked in the same fields for two or three hours, starting at 5 a.m. each morning from mid-April until the Fourth of July.

My own career path took me away from farm life. But I tried to involve our children in my work as much as possible. For example, while working for state government, I served in the crew that staged the opening of new sections of freeway. I remember taking our older son to one of these events, even introducing him to the governor of our state. During the years I led business-writing seminars, I paid the kids to collate pages and assemble them in three-ring binders.

Observing what you do at work provides a foundation for their own work lives in the years yet ahead of them.

Earning money has its spiritual hazards, dangers we need to take seriously (see chapter 12). But providing for your family year after year is yet another God-pleasing reason to get up and go to work.

Discussion

1. Describe any anxieties you, as a Christ-follower, may have about having money.
2. Why do you think God takes failure to support one's family so seriously?
3. In your household, who are those for whom you have financial responsibility?

For more: Chapter 4 of Hataj, Dave. *Good Work: How Blue Collar Business Can Change Lives, Communities, and the World*. Chicago: Moody, 2020.

19

Make Enough to Share

AFTER "NO!" WHAT IS one of first words toddlers learn to say?

Watch two of them as they are playing on the carpet. Kevin has been happily arranging his wooden blocks when Summer reaches over and grabs one. As he snatches it back, he aims one heated word at her: "Mine!"

Just as parents help their little ones to discover the world beyond "mine," God teaches his children to share. Our typical default position treats what we earn as belonging exclusively to ourselves and our loved ones.

When it comes to working for money, many people start out simply aiming to make enough to get by. If our income begins to bring in more than what we need to pay the bills, well . . . that's just a bonus. Extra money. No real plan for what to do with it. We can spend those dollars on our wish list.

Giving—A New Covenant Way of Life

Loving others by helping them financially provides yet another reason to get up and go to work. Plenty of New Testament teaching points us in this sharing direction. A few examples:

- Jesus himself teaches that giving to people suffering financial hardship somehow carries out within us a spiritual detox. "But now as for what is inside you—be generous to the poor, and everything will be clean for you" (Luke 11:41).
- Some Christians in first-century Ephesus were wealthy. In counseling Timothy on what they should do, Paul did not insist that they sell everything they had. Instead, he said, "Command them to do good, to be rich in good deeds, and to be generous and willing to share" (1 Tim 6:18).
- Over in Ephesus, some in the church (mimicking Jesus' disciple Judas) were apparently helping themselves to what belonged to others. Paul reminds them that living out the Christ-life within them means turning from taking to giving. "Anyone who has been stealing must steal no longer, but must work, doing something useful with their own hands, that they may have something to share with those in need" (Eph 4:28).
- The author of Hebrews admits that giving some of what we earn to others is a "sacrifice," a costly act—but one that delights the heart of God. "And do not forget to do good and to share with others, for with such sacrifices God is pleased" (Heb 13:16).

Giving—A Protection from Money's Power

Working exposes us to money, and money can damage us spiritually (see chapter 17). Giving away money, properly done, is one way to protect ourselves from such injury. But giving money to those outside our family needs to be seen through a new covenant lens.

In *The Other Six Days*, R. Paul Stevens lists mammon—"money that pretends to give security"[1]—as one of the "powers" spoken of in the New Testament. Surprisingly, though, these powers were not originally evil. They were created in and for Christ:

1. Stevens, *Other Six Days*, 220.

"For in him all things were created: things in heaven and on earth, visible and invisible, whether thrones or powers or rulers or authorities; all things have been created through him and for him" (Col 1:16).

But inside our fallen world-system, these powers act as if they were not accountable to their creator (Sound familiar? Echoes from Eden?). The powers, including mammon, exercise their clout in opposition to God. That explains why the money-power can so badly wound us spiritually.

Jesus, through his death and resurrection, has overcome the powers. He has "disarmed the powers . . . triumphing over them by the cross" (Col 2:15). And, as Stevens says, "This extraordinary ability of Jesus to overpower the powers is delegated to his followers."[2] Paul put it this way: "Therefore, if anyone is in Christ, the new creation has come: The old has gone, the new is here!" (2 Cor 5:17).

We Are Currency Converters

In the "new creation," Jesus has given us Christians the power to act as money converters. We have received the ability to turn mammon-currency into God's kingdom-currency. We can give the negative term "money-laundering" a new meaning. When money passes through our hands, we are to launder it, purge it of its evil power, and put it into uses that further the will of God being done on earth as in heaven.

It is extremely difficult to give away unconverted money. But once we convert it into a kingdom asset, we will see it as God's resource to do with as he directs.

Living as we do in the twenty-first century, how are we to translate first-century pictures of Christ-empowered giving into our own time and culture? Suppose our work brings home an income that rises above what it costs to support ourselves and our families. What would the Spirit of Christ lead us to do with the extra?

2. Stevens, *Other Six Days*, 227.

We may well ask ourselves:

- Where should our giving go? How are we to choose the recipients of our sharing?
- How should we give? Can some ways of giving actually harm the receivers?
- How much should we give? A tenth of our income? All of it?

Where to Give

Giving to the Poor

When it comes to sharing, God's heart has a clear first choice. The New Testament most often names the "poor" as his priority-receivers of our giving. The word for "poor" Jesus used when he said "the poor you will always have with you" includes beggars, the poverty-stricken, or—as we might say today—those who are dead broke.

Many of us—including me—do not regularly cross paths with people who live in dire economic poverty. Our hometown is situated in a county with a population of about 300,000. Officials say the homeless here in our county number between eight hundred and one thousand. That's about three-tenths of one percent, or one in three hundred people. So most of us seldom encounter the destitute in our daily life. How, then, can we share our working income with them?

Frequently we do see the poor at traffic intersections holding up cardboard signs that say things like "Out of work and hungry." A couple of years ago, my wife and I attended a graduation sponsored by our local Union Gospel Mission. The Mission operates men's and women's recovery programs for those addicted to drugs and alcohol—many of them who have lived on the street. When someone completes the program successfully, they are recognized in the graduation ceremony.

The evening concluded with a panel of four former "street people." The two hundred or so in the audience had an opportunity to direct questions to the panelists. One question was: "As Christians, what should we do when we see someone alongside the road with a cardboard sign asking for help?"

Following up on what the four said, I phoned our Union Gospel Mission and spoke with one of the panelists I'll call Karen—now working for the Mission. She told me that, while living on the street, she once had actually made a sign but was too embarrassed to go out and brazenly beg for money. Speaking from her experience of homelessness, she had some excellent suggestions for responding to the homeless on our street-corners:

1. *Pray.* When Karen sees someone on the street begging for help, she prays for discernment to know what to do. "If my heart leads me to give, then I do."
2. *Be ready.* You never know when you, as a driver or pedestrian, may encounter a homeless panhandler. Keep a few useful items in your car: maybe granola bars, socks, or toothbrushes. Recalling her days on the street, Karen said she often wished she could just brush her teeth.
3. *Never give money.* Except in rare circumstances, resist the urge to give money. Many of those begging for help are seeking cash for drugs. Some able-bodied people are making a business out of begging—and coming away with a fairly good living by doing so.
4. *Offer a meal ticket.* Karen told me our Union Gospel Mission provides vouchers that entitle the bearer to a hot meal. The ticket also offers hot showers, laundry facilities, a clothing bank, and advertises a church service.

"Send me a supply of tickets," I said to Karen. She did, and we have begun using them. The very location of their facilities puts Karen and others in the Union Gospel Mission in regular contact with the homeless. By regularly supporting the Mission financially, we help to make the hot meals and other services possible.

Much essential work gets done by those who labor outside the for-profit marketplace. What these workers do is indispensable if life is to flourish on earth in the twenty-first century. And because God calls for our giving to them, such giving provides yet another motivation to get up and go to work.

Giving to Those in Gospel-Extension Work

Some Christians spend their time in what we might call "gospel-extension" tasks. These efforts would include evangelism and disciple-making. Teaching and preaching are work. Those God calls into vocational ministry roles have a God-given right to be paid for their labor. As Paul wrote, "The Lord has commanded that those who preach the gospel should receive their living from the gospel" (1 Cor 9:14).

The Message paraphrase says: "Give a bonus to leaders who do a good job, especially the ones who work hard at preaching and teaching. Scripture tells us, 'Don't muzzle a working ox,' and, 'A worker deserves his wages'" (1 Tim 5:17–18).

Some who do gospel work choose to support themselves by working in other fields. Paul made his living in the tent-manufacturing business. Yet from time to time he did receive financial gifts from the churches he served.

Giving to Need-Meeting Organizations

In addition to those in gospel-extension work, some work in organizations whose purpose is to meet a variety of pressing needs. For example, Water Mission is a "Christian engineering nonprofit that builds safe water, sanitation, and hygiene solutions in developing countries and disaster areas."[3] The Mercy Ships[4] organization deploys hospital ships to provide access to safe surgery and medical care for people of all ages. Pioneer Bible Translators explain

3. Water Mission, "Our Solutions."

4. Mercy Ships, "Who We Are."

that they do their work "to disciple the Bibleless, mobilizing God's people to provide enduring access to God's word. Our vision is to see transformed lives through God's word in every language."[5]

The efforts of people in organizations like these fit what Scripture says: "As we have opportunity, let us do good to all people, especially to those who belong to the family of believers" (Gal 6:10). The gospel summons us not only to church-related activity but also to work for the wellbeing of everyone.

Giving to Support God's Government Workers

Now for a go-to-work motive many have never seen as a giving opportunity: paying taxes. Taxation takes many forms—income tax, property tax, sales tax, and so on. Government employees are non-marketplace workers. Money for their wages and salaries comes from those who work in the for-profit work world.

Without the work of those in government, we would not have roads, highways, and freeways. No fire departments, no police protection, no public schools, no retirement benefits, and more. In Bible times, Joseph worked for the Egyptian government and Daniel worked for the Babylonian government. Each helped to maintain an environment in which life on earth could flourish.

Paul explains that we pay taxes because "the authorities are God's servants, who give their full time to governing" (Rom 13:6) The God who says "The worker deserves his wages" (1 Tim 5:18) provides for those who serve him in government roles. It follows, then, that "if you owe taxes, pay taxes" (Rom 13:7).

How to Give

After converting mammon-money into kingdom-currency, we should be wise in the way we invest God's money. Fortunately, we now have access to websites that will help us see whether this or that organization is using responsibly the money given to it.

5. Pioneer Bible Translators, "Transformed Lives through God's Word."

For example, by keying the name of an organization into Charity Navigator or Guidestar.org, you can get a quick assessment of how a charitable organization spends its funds.

When giving to individuals rather than organizations, it may help to keep in mind the now-famous eight levels of giving named by Moses ben Maimon in the twelfth century. This Jewish philosopher/physician/rabbi taught what some have called the "ladder" of giving. He began with the least beneficial way to give and ended with the best way to do it. Here is my paraphrase of his ladder:[6]

- Level 8. You give while gritting your teeth.
- Level 7. You give a little bit—but with a grin.
- Level 6. You give if someone begs you to.
- Level 5. You give to poor people, even if they don't ask.
- Level 4. You get credit for giving, but don't know the receivers.
- Level 3. You give when both you and the receiver remain anonymous.
- Level 2. You give to a common fund that other people distribute.
- Level 1. (Best of all) You give in a way that (a) provides generous help that preserves the receiver's dignity, or (b) extends a loan that fits the situation, or (c) helps the receiver get a job or set up a business of their own.

How Much to Give?

A great many of us have been taught that the tithe—one-tenth of our income—is to be given to our local church. I have heard this verse quoted to support that idea: "Bring the whole tithe into the storehouse" (Mal 3:10). But does this old covenant command apply to New Testament Christ followers?

6. Maimonides, "Maimonides' Eight Levels of Charity."

The storehouse back then was a chamber in the temple where God's people brought grain, wine, and oil for use by the Levites. Nothing today compares with that "storehouse." Nor do we have any Levites in the new covenant.

A popular idea is that the old covenant tithe amounted to ten percent. However, because the Law required the Israelites to give multiple tithes—perhaps twelve or fourteen times over a seven-year period—the total was far more than ten percent. Gospel Coalition writer Thomas Schreiner says, "In fact, the number was probably somewhere around 20 percent per year."[7]

The New Testament does not prescribe any amount for giving by new covenant believers. Instead of being directed by a giving rule we are to be guided by the Holy Spirit through our new and generous hearts. As Paul told the Christians in Corinth, "Each of you should give what you have decided in your heart to give, not reluctantly or under compulsion, for God loves a cheerful giver" (2 Cor 9:7).

A personal note: Rather than looking at the old covenant tithe as a rule to follow, I use it as a historically useful reference point. The Israelites were required to give their tithes. They lived under the law. Now, in the age of the outpoured Spirit, I check myself by asking: Would God lead me to give less than they were expected to give?

Giving as Motivation to Work

So as Christians, our giving can go to the poor and to non-marketplace workers—such as gospel-extension workers, to organizations that meet various needs, and to God's servants in government agencies. As Christians, maybe each of us should ask ourselves, "What if I were to make it my goal to bring home more than I and my family need—enough to give away?

7. Schreiner, "7 Reasons Christians Are Not Required to Tithe."

That would add—in addition to those in previous chapters—yet one more good reason to get up and serve God day after day by going to work.

Discussion

1. How are you doing as a currency converter for the kingdom of God?
2. Where do you find it the easiest to give? The most difficult? Why?
3. What changes, if any, do you think God is calling to make in your giving pattern?

For more: Chapter 9 of Gill, David. *Workplace Discipleship 101: A Primer*. Peabody, MA: Hendrickson, 2020.

Epilogue

THESE CHAPTERS HAVE, I hope, explained why God loves your work. When we realize that the good God has put something he prizes into our hands, how should we respond?

Gratitude is a good place to begin. God was under no obligation to share with us the privilege of helping to care for his earth and all he had put within it. He has revealed himself to be more than capable of creating, sustaining, repairing, cleaning, and so on. But he did not see the care and responsibility for his earth as something to be kept only for himself. Because we have received such a valuable gift, the fitting response is "Thank you!"

Giving thanks for our work immediately puts us in territory quite distant from so many in the work world. As mentioned earlier in this book, around two-thirds of employees are either disengaged or actively disengaged with their work. Several years ago, Al Sharpton hosted a TV series called *I Hate My Job*. Johnny Paycheck wrote a song he called "Take This Job and Shove It."

But when we are doing something we know God loves, we can throw ourselves into it wholeheartedly. The discovery that God has many purposes for sending us to work makes getting up and going to work a great deal easier. Those purposes offer us many reasons to be grateful when we realize that:

- Obeying God, once seen as what we do in a church setting during our off-hours, now becomes our week-long privilege. We can obey him even while programming a computer, splinting a pet's broken leg, or bagging groceries.
- God has made us his partners, his coworkers, in maintaining life on his beautiful planet earth. This dignifies us—something like being asked by the president to serve in an administrative office in the government to help carry out what is good.
- Even the inevitable pressures and stresses of work—the "thorns and thistles"—have eternal meaning. Through them, God is reshaping us to become more and more like his Son.
- We can have a ministry of encouragement to other believers in our work circles—coworkers, customers, patients, students, etc. And we can do this on weekdays, not just in our spare time.
- Our witness becomes far more than simply speaking the gospel to non-Christians. Because the Spirit of Christ lives in us, we can embody the truth, making Jesus known through the way we act, interact, and react in all kinds of work circumstances.
- God intends that some of the money we earn in our work be used to support ourselves and our families. Self-support is not selfishness.
- We can aim to earn even more than we need to bring in funds to share with the poor, with those in gospel-extension vocations, with need-meeting organizations, and—through paying taxes—with those who serve God in government.

But our daily work is only part of the gratitude landscape. One more reason to give thanks is for God's provision of rest from our labors. He has built into our DNA the need for a work-rest rhythm patterned after his own work and rest at creation and after his freeing the Israelites from their slave work.

Who might you know who would benefit from the truth about work presented in these pages? Consider these possibilities:

- A young person who will soon enter the world of work.
- Someone who has just begun their working career and wants to know how to offer their work as worship.
- A seasoned worker who thinks they may have missed God's calling by engaging in so-called "secular work."
- A stay-at-home parent who needs to know that God prizes their unpaid work.
- A pastor or church leader who can benefit their congregation by teaching the biblical truth about work.

Perhaps you can help working Christians to stop sighing "Thank God it's Friday" and begin saying "Thank God, it's time again to get up and go to work!" Encourage them to bring into their prayers something Moses prayed: "And let the loveliness of our Lord, our God, rest on us, confirming the work that we do. Oh, yes. Affirm the work that we do!" (Ps 90:17, MSG).

Bibliography

4Laws.com. "Four Spiritual Laws." http://www.4laws.com/laws/englishkgp/default.htm.

ACFE. "2020 Global Fraud Study—Key Findings." https://acfepublic.s3-us-west-2.amazonaws.com/2020-Report-to-the-Nations.pdf.

Bakke, Dennis. *Joy at Work: A Revolutionary Approach to Fun on the Job*. Seattle: PVG, 2005.

Banks, Robert. *God the Worker: Journeys into the Mind, Heart, and Imagination of God*. Eugene, OR: Wipf & Stock, 2008.

Bernbaum, John A., and Simon M. Steer. *Why Work: Careers and Employment in Biblical Perspective*. Grand Rapids, MI: Baker, 1986.

Bible Hub. "Question of the Comparison Between the Active and the Contemplative Life." https://biblehub.com/library/aquinas/on_prayer_and_the_contemplative_life/question_clxxxii_of_the_comparison.htm.

Biffot-Lacout, Sandra. "'Open Bar' for Rats as Paris Pension Strikes Hit Waste Collection." *Yahoo News* February 3, 2020. https://www.yahoo.com/now/open-bar-rats-paris-pension-strikes-hit-waste-165709243.html?guccounter=1.

Black, Bob. "The Abolition of Work." https://theanarchistlibrary.org/library/bob-black-the-abolition-of-work/.

Borneman, Adam. "The Justice of Sabbath." *The Ministry Collaborative* July 28, 2016. https://mministry.org/the-justice-of-sabbath/.

Brooks, David. "The Gender War Is On! And Fake." https://www.nytimes.com/2018/07/02/opinion/gender-war-voting-equality-economics-family.html.

Brueggemann, Walter. *Genesis*. Louisville: John Knox, 2010.

Bureau of Labor Statistics. "Usual Weekly Earnings of Wage and Salary Workers Third Quarter 2021." https://www.bls.gov/news.release/pdf/wkyeng.pdf.

CRIEnglish.com. "600,000 Chinese Die from Overworking Each Year." *China Daily* December 11, 2016. http://www.chinadaily.com.cn/china/2016-12/11/content_27635578.htm.

Comer, John Mark. *Garden City*. Grand Rapids, MI: Zondervan, 2015.

Cosden, Darell. *The Heavenly Good of Earthly Work*. Peabody, MA: Hendrickson, 2006.

DeKoster, Lester. *Work: The Meaning of Your Life*. Grand Rapids, MI: Christian's Library, 1982.

Del Junco, Paul. "The Curse of Work." https://sojo.net/magazine/march-april-1997/curse-work.

Eberstadt, Nicholas. *Men without Work: America's Invisible Crisis*. West Conshohocken, PA: Templeton, 2016.

Eldred, Ken. *The Integrated Life: Experience the Powerful Advantage of Integrating Your FAITH and WORK*. Montrose, CO: Manna Ventures, 2010.

Elliot, Elizabeth. *Discipline: The Glad Surrender*. Grand Rapids, MI: Fleming H. Revell, 2006.

Eng, Faith. "20 Inspiring Bible Verses about God's Amazing Love for You." https://www.cru.org/us/en/train-and-grow/spiritual-growth/gods-love-scriptures.html.

Faith and Work Movement. "Our Story." https://www.faithandworkmovement.org/about.

Geisler, Norman L., and Rady Douglass. *Integrity at Work: Finding Your Ethical Compass in a Post-Enron World*. Ada, MI: Baker, 2007.

Gill, David. *Doing Right: Practicing Ethical Principles*. Downers Grove, IL: InterVarsity, 2004.

———. *Workplace Discipleship 101: A Primer*. Peabody, MA: Hendrickson, 2020.

Goodreads. "Martin Luther." https://www.goodreads.com/quotes/924405-the-christian-shoemaker-does-his-duty-not-by-putting-little.

———. "Stanley Hauerwas." https://www.goodreads.com/quotes/822392-my-father-was-a-better-bricklayer-than-i-am-a.

———. "Steve Jobs." https://www.goodreads.com/quotes/772887-the-only-way-to-do-great-work-is-to-love.

Greear, J. D. "Martin Luther on the 'Masks of God.'" https://jdgreear.com/martin-luther-on-gods-masks/.

Green, Alison. "I Hate Work, All of It, with a Passion." https://www.askamanager.org/2015/03/i-hate-work-all-of-it-with-a-passion.html.

Greene, Mark. "Sacred Secular Divide." *Youtube*. https://www.youtube.com/watch?v=wgDLzINl9mI.

Harter, Jim. "US Employee Engagement Rises Following Wild 2020." *Gallup* February 26, 2021. https://www.gallup.com/workplace/330017/employee-engagement-rises-following-wild-2020.aspx.

Hataj, Dave. *Good Work: How Blue Collar Business Can Change Lives, Communities, and the World*. Chicago: Moody, 2020.

Kaemingk, Matthew, and Corey B. Willson. *Work and Worship: Reconnecting Our Labor and Liturgy*. Ada, MI: Baker Academic, 2020.

Keller, Timothy, and Katherine Leary Alsdorf. *Every Good Endeavor: Connecting Your Work to God's Work*. New York: Penguin, 2016.

The Ken Coleman Show. "I Go to Work in Tears Every Day Because I Hate My Job!" *Youtube*. https://www.youtube.com/watch?v=qAhmqapFj9A.

Kincade, Shawn. "The Futility of Pushing a String . . ." https://aspirekc.com/the-futility-of-pushing-a-string/.

Knapp, John C. *How the Church Fails Businesspeople: And What Can Be Done about It*. Grand Rapids, MI: Eerdmans, 2012.

Kohl, Art. "Should a Christian Mother Work outside the Home?" https://www.thechristianwoman.com/christian-women-topics/should-christian-mother-work.

Kowalczuk, Ruth. *I Came Only For English* . . . Maitland, FL: Xulon, 2021.

Kumar, Kamalini. "Work as Worship." https://worklife.org/2020/09/17/work-as-worship/.

LaGravenese, Richard, dir. *Freedom Writers*. Hollywood, CA: MTV Films, 2007.

Lapp, C. W. "Born a Man, Died _________." https://cwlapp.com/2016/05/26/born-a-man-died-_________/.

Larimore, Walt. "Employed by God." *Focus on the Family* October 22, 2014. https://www.focusonthefamily.com/faith/employed-by-god/.

Lexico. "Meaning of Sacred in English." https://www.lexico.com/definition/sacred.

———. "Meaning of Secular in English." https://www.lexico.com/definition/secular.

Maimonides. "Maimonides' Eight Levels of Charity." *Chabad.org*. https://www.chabad.org/library/article_cdo/aid/45907/jewish/Eight-Levels-of-Charity.htm.

Mercy Ships. "Who We Are." https://www.mercyships.org/.

Merriam-Webster Online. "Work." https://www.merriam-webster.com/dictionary/work.

Miller, Darrow L. *LifeWork: A Biblical Theology for What You Do Every Day*. Seattle: YWAM, 2009.

Morse, Anne. "When I Grow Up, I Want to Be . . ." https://www.boundless.org/adulthood/when-i-grow-up-i-want-to-be/.

Murray, Andrew. *Abide in Christ*. Fort Washington, PA: Christian Literature Crusade, 1963.

Nelson, Tom. "Work Matters: Connecting Sunday Worship to Monday Work." *Youtube*. https://www.youtube.com/watch?v=V9caqPr7ExI.

Nowlen, Jonathan. *Managing Your Metron: A Practical Theology of Work, Mission, and Meaning*. Self-published, 2019.

Oates, Wayne E. *Confessions of a Workaholic*. Cleveland: World, 1971.

Ostsring, Elizabeth Ellen. *Be a Blessing: The Theology of Work in the Narrative of Genesis*. Eugene, OR: Wipf & Stock, 2016.

Overman, Christian. *God's Pleasure at Work: Bridging the Sacred-Secular Divide*. Bellevue, WA: Ablaze, 2009.

Padilla, Kristen. "'All Work Is God's Work' New York Times Bestseller Tim Keller Tells Samford Crowd." https://www.samford.edu/news/2016/11/All-work-is-God-work-New-York-Times-Bestseller-Tim-Keller-Tells-Samford-Crowd.

Peabody, Larry. *Job-Shadowing Daniel: Walking the Talk at Work*. Denver: Outskirts, 2010.

———. *Serving Christ in the Workplace: Secular Work Is Full-Time Service*. Peabody, MA: Christian Literature Crusade, 1974.

Petersen, Randy. "Modern Voices: The Christian and Money." *Christianity Today*. https://www.christianitytoday.com/history/issues/issue-14/modern-voices-christian-and-money.html.

Peterson, Eugene H. *Christ Plays in Ten Thousand Places: A Conversation in Spiritual Theology*. Grand Rapids, MI: Eerdmans, 2008.

Pioneer Bible Translators. "Transformed Lives through God's Word in Every Language." https://pioneerbible.org/.

Reed, Jonathan, and John Dominic Crossan. "The First-Century Galilee Boat." https://www.bibleodyssey.org/en/people/related-articles/first-century-galilee-boat.

Rees, D. Vaughan. *The "Jesus Family" in Communist China*. London: Paternoster, 1959.

RightNow Media. "Workaholic." https://www.rightnowmedia.org/Content/illustration/103601.

Sarah, "Why Is It So Hard to Give Yourself Permission to Rest?" *Pomegranite* March 15, 2018. https://www.pomegranite.co.za/why-is-it-so-hard-to-give-yourself-permission-to-rest/.

Sayers, Dorothy. "Why Work?" https://tnl.org/wp-content/uploads/Why-Work-Dorothy-Sayers.pdf.

Schreiner, Thomas. "7 Reasons Christians Are Not Required to Tithe." https://www.thegospelcoalition.org/article/7-reasons-christians-not-required-to-tithe/.

Sengupta, Agnipravo. "7 Greek Gods and Goddesses You Need To Avoid As Work Colleagues." https://www.business2community.com/human-resources/7-greek-gods-goddesses-need-avoid-work-colleagues-01147389.

Sherman, Amy L. *Kingdom Calling: Vocational Stewardship for the Common Good*. Downers Grove, IL: InterVarsity, 2011.

Sherman, Doug, and William Hendricks. *Your Work Matters to God*. Colorado Springs: Navpress, 1987.

———. *Your Work Matters to God: A Study Guide on the Best-Selling Book*. Colorado Springs: NavPress, 1988.

Simmons, Gina. "Mad as Hell and Stealing from Employers." *Forbes* October 25, 2011. https://www.forbes.com/sites/crime/2011/10/25/mad-as-hell-and-stealing-from-employers/?sh=5870e1e13732.

Stevens, R. Paul. *The Other Six Days*. Grand Rapids, MI: Eerdmans, 2016.

Stott, John R. W. *Issues Facing Christians Today*. Grand Rapids, MI: Zondervan, 2011.

Terkel, Studs. *Working: People Talk about What They Do All Day and How They Feel about What They Do*. New York: New Press, 2004.

Tournier, Paul. *Fatigue in Modern Society*. Louisville: John Knox, 1978.

Tozer, A. W. *Man, the Dwelling Place of God*. Virginia Beach: Createspace, 2009.

Van Duzer, Jeff. *Why Business Matters to God (And What Still Needs to Be Fixed)*. Downers Grove, IL: InterVarsity, 2010.

Water Mission. "Our Solutions." https://watermission.org/our-solutions/where-we-work/.

Whelchel, Hugh. "The Historical Influences of the Sacred-Secular Divide." https://tifwe.org/historical-influences-of-the-sacred-secular-divide/.

Willard, Dallas. *The Divine Conspiracy: Rediscovering Our Hidden Life in God*. San Francisco: HarperSanFrancisco, 2014.

———. *The Spirit of the Disciplines: Understanding How God Changes Lives*. New York: HarperOne, 2001.

Wright, N. T. *How God Became King: The Forgotten Story of the Gospels*. New York: HarperOne, 2016.

Zuckerman, Arthur. "39 Employee Theft Statistics: 2020/2021 Impact and Costs to Business." https://comparecamp.com/employee-theft-statistics/.